The Future of Religion

The Future of Religion

Edited by

Paul Rennick, Stanley Cunningham
and Ralph H. Johnson

BL
60
.F885
2010

The Future of Religion,
Edited by Paul Rennick, Stanley Cunningham and Ralph H. Johnson

This book first published 2010

Cambridge Scholars Publishing

12 Back Chapman Street, Newcastle upon Tyne, NE6 2XX, UK

British Library Cataloguing in Publication Data
A catalogue record for this book is available from the British Library

Copyright © 2010 by Paul Rennick, Stanley Cunningham
and Ralph H. Johnson and contributors

All rights for this book reserved. No part of this book may be reproduced, stored in a retrieval system, or transmitted, in any form or by any means, electronic, mechanical, photocopying, recording or otherwise, without the prior permission of the copyright owner.

ISBN (10): 1-4438-1972-7, ISBN (13): 978-1-4438-1972-5

Dedicated to the Basilian Fathers
who have nourished Assumption University
since its earliest days

TABLE OF CONTENTS

Preface ix

Foreword 1
Reflections on Religion and the Future
Charles Kimball

PART I: RELIGION AND THE PUBLIC FORUM 17

Chapter One 19
Religion, Law and Politics
Moira McQueen

Chapter Two 27
Neither Naked nor Sacred: Religion in the Public Square
Carol Stanton

PART II: RELIGION AND SCIENCE 47

Chapter Three 49
Darwinism vs. Intelligent Design in a Religious Context
Dennis Hudecki

Chapter Four 67
Science, Religion and the Illusion of Certainty
Donald J. Lococo C.S.B.

PART III: RELIGION AND COMMUNICATION 81

Chapter Five 83
Reflections on the Interface between Propaganda and Religion
Stanley B. Cunningham

Chapter Six 97
Feeding the Soul: Food, Television and Faith
Renée Bondy

PART IV: RELIGION AND MODERNITY 107

Chapter Seven 109
The Uneasy Alliance: The Ongoing Relationship between Philosophy and Religion
Ralph H. Johnson

Chapter Eight 129
Islam and Modernity
Mohammad Sadegh Zahedi

Afterword 139
Recent Developments in Perspectives on Religion
Gregory Baum

Contributors 155

PREFACE

Just over eight decades ago, in 1927, Sigmund Freud published his valediction to religion: *The Future of an Illusion*. Using the perspectives of psychoanalysis, Freud reduced religion to an illusion and opined that science would soon make religion unnecessary.

Freud was among the most influential thinkers of the 20th century, a century that has achieved world changing advances in science. Yet, at the beginning of the 21st century, religion has not only not disappeared or been reduced to insignificance; rather, it has become one of the most vigorous forces in contemporary geopolitics. Ironically, the awareness of the power of religion, on a global scale, is, in part, a consequence of the technological developments of the last century, the very developments that some thought would render religion inconsequential.

Religion admits of many definitions. Generally, here, we can say that religion is a meaning system that addresses the issues of ultimate meaning, or transcendent meaning. When this ultimate or transcendent meaning is named as "God" the dynamic we call "religion" takes a theistic turn, and moves toward the development of creeds, codes of conduct, rituals and that whole panoply of activities and dispositions that are the elements by which we normally identify religion. But the realm of *ultimate meaning* is the *foundation* of religion and only in this context, we submit, can the sustained power of religion be fully comprehended.

While the progress of the last century has not obviated the purpose and need for religion, the 20th century did manifest some of the dangers and consequences of religious distortions in various cultures, and thus, by contrast, the proper functions of religion in healthy societies.

The Interaction of Religion and Culture

The role of religion in culture has a varied history. Beyond the particulars of specific historical situations, religion, it seems, has the capacity to provide culture with an internally rooted self-critical, self-correcting capacity. It is religion's role to present the possibility of self-transcendence to individuals and societies. In doing this, religion endows culture with an expanded cultural consciousness of what it means to be human, and thereby enhances the human enterprise of personal and social development. This can be most clearly seen when religion is denied its proper role in the culture.

When a society becomes *officially atheistic* and religion is legally and forcibly excised from the life of the culture there is a marked diminishment of human standards and of the value of human persons. In fact, there is a diminishment of productivity and prosperity on almost every level, save possibly for a few select projects or people.

While the former Union of Soviet Socialist Republics might be the most prominent example of this situation, it is not the only socio-political entity that has followed this route. Those who have lived under such atheistic regimes speak, not simply of the diminishment of human development, but of its destruction.

Similarly, when a society becomes *officially theistic* or *theocratic,* human, personal and social development are again diminished. In a theocracy, religion controls the culture rather than being a source of renewal or self-reflection within a culture. When this happens, the culture is narrowed down to a single, historically-conditioned perspective, which, it is said (by some demagogue), is God's perspective of what humanity ought to look like and how it ought to behave. And since the source for this perspective is religiously derived, it is perceived to have a sacred quality. This sacred quality imposes a supposedly divine imprint on, what is in fact, a limited, historically conditioned perspective. In a theocracy the culture rapidly fossilizes into rigid and righteously defined modes.

We can see this in the Islamic Republic of Iran where the Supreme Leader is a cleric who is not elected but holds the authority that his title indicates. While there is a parallel democratic structure, with a President, Prime Minister, electoral processes etc., at its core, Iran is governed by Islam. Iran is not the only country that would call itself a Muslim state, and many of them are basically theocracies. It is important to remember, however, that there is nothing intrinsic to Islam that would make this the only model by which Moslems participate in the political realm.

When religion neither dominates nor is dismissed, it gives voice to a dimension of humanity that summons the culture to foster increasingly the conditions for ever greater human dignity, freedom and creativity. Again, in the 20th century, the human rights movement is an example of how religion has historically contributed to the development of the culture's understanding of what it is to be human. Historians agree that the civil rights movement for racial equality in the United States could not have succeeded without religion and the institutions that maintain the religious dimension.

Recently among the rash of publications on religion is the voice of a militant atheism, at least among English readership (Harris, *The End of Faith*, 2002; Dawkins, *The God Delusion*, 2006; Dennett, *Breaking the Spell*, 2006; Onfrey, *In Defence of Atheism: The Case Against Christianity, Judaism, and Islam* 2007; Stenger, *God the Failed Hypothesis*, 2007; Hitchens, *god is not Great*, 2007). While this voice does not come from any governmental or juridical authority, it may be an indicator of a perspective emerging from other levels of the culture. This perspective identifies religion as the problem, and calls for the elimination of religion as the solution. It is, however, an inadequate analysis of the current geo-political situation in which the enormous variety of cultures, meanings, religions and systems, discloses to us the pluralistic nature of human reality and with which ordinary people must now contend in their everyday lives. We have truly become a "global village," and now we must learn how to live in such proximity.

Pluralism

Pluralism can be defined as the moral, intellectual or societal framework that allows for a variety of approaches to living communally, democratically and peacefully. This describes what we can call social pluralism, while religious pluralism refers not just to "a variety of approaches," but *contending* approaches at the *level of ultimate meaning*.

This is the situation in which we, in first-world Western culture, find ourselves today and which is referenced by the terms "post-modernism" and "deconstructionism." There is no single over-arching meta-narrative that commands the total assent of the culture. This is not merely an academic matter; it is also one that determines the degree to which shared meaning grounds the notion of the common good on which human society is built. When shared meaning is eroded, the common ground on which we stand is not simply shaken, it collapses. Symptomatic of this collapse are the relativism and radical subjectivism that many uncritically assume are the sole approach in the business of discerning the good, the true, the responsible, and the meaningful way of life.

There is an easy eclecticism that masquerades as pluralism, but as contemporary American Catholic theologian David Tracy comments: *authentic pluralism expects conflict and demands dialogue*. Conflict is intrinsic to pluralism because there is variety and difference at the deepest levels and about the deepest values. Dialogue is necessary to make authentic pluralism viable, to make these fundamental variations sources of diversity rather than sources of division. Without a robust dialogue we can easily degenerate into the lowest common-denominator mentality which is insufficient to hold together the complexities of modern society and to keep them intact.

It is precisely this dialogue that a society needs at every level, including the academy, and yet it seems to be lacking. Where we should find and foster communication we see excommunication. We are awash in information without any coherent centre to bring it and us together. Indeed, the possibility of a coherent synthesis, and the people who search for such synthesis, are viewed with suspicion.

Yet, it is a mistake to see pluralism as the problem, which many "religious" perspectives seem to do. The problem is the absence of dialogue and the lack of protocols for how such a dialogue might proceed. And although the university may be no less shattered than the rest of the culture, it remains an important forum where this conversation must happen, even when there is no sure and clear path forward.

As part of an attempt to foster this dialogue, Assumption University, Windsor, Canada as part of its 150th anniversary celebrations in 2007 decided to hold an international conference addressing *The Future of Religion*. (The echo of Freud's title from 80 years previous was purposeful.) This volume, containing some of the papers presented at this conference, now extends the dialogue to a wider audience.

Dr. Charles Kimball, whose timely publication *When Religion Becomes Evil* (2002) addressed so many of the issues surfacing around religion, was invited to be the conference keynote speaker and kindly allowed his address to be part of this collection. Also, the internationally prominent Canadian theologian, Dr. Gregory Baum, agreed to provide an endnote address that is also included. Between these two scholars are eight presentations by scholars from various disciplines. These papers are grouped together under four headings: Religion and the Public Forum; Religion and Science; Religion and Communication; and Religion and Modernity.

We see this volume as an initial offering rather than as something exhaustive, and hope that this modest contribution to the dialogue will be of assistance, both in charting the future for religion and for our shared human community.

—The Editors
Windsor, Ontario
2010

FOREWORD

REFLECTIONS ON RELIGION AND THE FUTURE[*]

CHARLES KIMBALL

Two years ago, I was at a conference of Jewish and Christian leaders. There were about 16 of us. We were virtually locked into a room for about three days where we wrestled with the question: What is the future of relations, not just between Jews and Christians, but increasingly between Jewish, Christian, and Muslim communities? At one particularly pointed moment, one of the rabbis cleared his throat, got all of our attention and said: "My friends, the next 10 years will be the most difficult…they always have been!" Indeed, the next 10 years always have been the most difficult, but in the context in which we are operating today, our future prospects are complicated by some new features: In addition to a volatile mix of religion and politics, which I will be talking about, we also have to take into account the dynamics of pluralism and interdependence.

The world has always been religiously diverse—that's not new. What is new is our awareness of this diversity, not just globally but increasingly at the local level as well. Our growing awareness of our interdependence in all sorts of ways tells us that we really are in this together globally, nationally, locally, in some very dramatic ways. We see this every day in the news, but increasingly the dynamics are visible at the local level in the United States and Canada. We needn't look any further than Windsor or Vancouver, Toronto or Montreal, or across the river to Dearborn, Michigan to get the point rather quickly. The landscape is changing in the 21st century; we face challenges, and they are urgent.

We've learned a lot in the years since September 11, 2001. In many ways we're still learning, but I would suggest that there are three things that we can all readily agree that we have learned in the years since those

---

[*] This paper was originally given as a keynote address. The Editors decided to keep the colloquial, informal tone in reproducing the paper for this book.

horrific events. One is that religion is an extraordinarily powerful force in human society, and always has been. Religion has inspired people to their highest and noblest best. Throughout human history, some of the greatest things that human beings have done have been done in the name of religion, or they have been inspired by believers' faith in various religious communities. At the same time, we know all too well that religion has been a force for destructive behaviour or at least has been used as a justification by people for violent and destructive behaviour, again within various religious traditions. Religion is a very powerful force, and sometimes that force devolves into violent and destructive purposes.

A second thing that we have now learned is that the world is awash in weapons of mass destruction. We knew this before, but we know it now with sobering clarity. We all knew that there were chemical, nuclear, and biological weapons in the former Soviet Union stockpiles, but on September 10, 2001, few of us yet were desperately concerned about what exactly was happening with those weapons. We assumed somebody was paying attention, that somebody was minding the store. After 9/11, we realized that we can no longer make those assumptions. There are people in the world who want to get their hands on weapons of mass destruction, and will pay a great price to get them and use them against others to pursue whatever their goals are.

At a deeper level, part of what was so shocking and what we live with all the time is that the world is also full of other kinds of weapons of mass destruction to which we had given less thought. The bombing in Oklahoma City and the events of September 11 did not employ chemical, nuclear or biological weapons. Fertilizer was the weapon of mass destruction in Oklahoma City, and the hijackers of September 11 used box knives and a clever plan to turn commercial airliners into new weapons of mass destruction. In other words, there are all kinds of ways that people can do great harm when their intent is to do great harm—quite apart from whether they get their hands on biological or chemical weapons. This is a third thing on which we can agree, and when you put these three points of agreement together, what really underscores the urgency is that we now know with certainty that it takes only a very few people to wreak havoc on a global scale.

I will be referring more extensively to Islam later, but one thing I would like to indicate here is that in my experience of well over 30 years of studying Islam, living in the Middle East, knowing many Muslims and knowing many people who study Islam, the vast majority of Muslims all over the world are horrified and offended by the acts of violent extremists in the same way that all of us Westerners are. There are many people in various countries who are angry and frustrated for different reasons. Again, that's not the subject of my presentation. But if we explore the reasons for discontent, I argue in a number of books and articles that most of us, were we caught in those same circumstances, born in countries where there was such economic exploitation and human rights violation and political repression—given all that, we too would be just as angry and frustrated. Granted that there's a great deal of anger and frustration out there, that's still a very different thing than people who have reached the point of desperation and act out their violent extremism, often in acts of suicidal self-sacrifice.

My own introduction to religious diversity and pluralism began in childhood. The wonderful story depicted in *Fiddler on the Roof* is very much the story of a big part of my family. My great-grandfather was an Orthodox Jewish cantor who came from the Poland-Russia corridor. His was one of those families forced out in a Christian pogrom against the Jews. The family then immigrated to the United States and settled in the Boston area. My grandfather, one of nine children in this family, and one of his brothers began singing and dancing for pennies on the street corners of Boston. They were good, and took their show on the road and eventually became a famous song-and-dance comedy team on the vaudeville circuit. They travelled to Europe and Australia, all over the world. As a child growing up in this period, my father was often on trains, with The Three Stooges in the compartment next door. Charlie Chaplin, one of my grandfather's best friends, tried to get him to go into silent movies but Grandpa said "No, no, movies will never go anywhere. I'll stick with vaudeville, that's the sure thing." He wound up selling dental supplies in Tulsa, Oklahoma, while Charlie Chaplin, as it turned out, moved on to a different career.

During his days in vaudeville, my grandfather met and married my grandmother who was a chorus girl in the show and also a Presbyterian. Neither ever converted to the other's religion, so I grew up in Tulsa, Oklahoma, with a Jewish grandfather and a Presbyterian grandmother. My father and his brothers all became Christians, but it was really only a little pocket of the family out there in Oklahoma. The larger, extended family, comprising hundreds of second and third cousins, were all Jewish. I grew up thinking of, and being taught and experiencing, Judaism as something very good. What my parents taught me and what my experience taught me was that yes, we are Christians but it's also good to be Jewish: not just O.K. to be Jewish, but *good* to be Jewish. However, about the time I entered the third grade I discovered that not everybody else in Tulsa shared that same view. I didn't yet know the term "anti-

Semitism," but that was what I was beginning to hear from kids on the playground and street corners who had never met anybody Jewish, and who were just repeating what they had heard from parents and others. So, at an early age, I began to experience what racism and bigotry are, and not surprisingly, as a child, I took that as a personal assault on my own grandfather, the most wonderful person I knew. I tell you this story to explain why, from an early age, there has always been deep within me this question that I think we all wrestle with in different ways: What does it mean to be a person of faith—in my case, a Christian—in a world where my early experience clearly did not exhaust all the possibilities? Surely God must be greater than just my experience of God.

At some level, I knew what we all know: that had I been born in another part of my own family, I would have been Jewish. If I had been born in Tehran instead of Tulsa, I would have been raised as a Muslim. Now, to the best of my knowledge I didn't pick Tulsa and you didn't pick Iran as your place of birth. So where does God figure in all of this, and how do we make sense of it all? Our diversity continues to animate me as a student of world religions. Operating within the Christian context, I am very much interested in exploring these kinds of questions.

As already mentioned, I spent a great deal of my professional life working both in the Middle East as well as in the academic world, engaged in many of the situations that figure so prominently in the news. Political changes are happening all around us, sometimes in dramatic and violent ways. We see, too, that in many ways in our world of nation states, religion and various forms of democracy interestingly are often central factors. What is going on, we ask, and where do we find hope in the perilous journey that seems to lie ahead? A wise friend once observed that when you're standing on the edge of a cliff, progress is not defined as one step forward. I think that's a good thing to bear in mind. Perhaps, what we need to do is take a step or two back to gain a better perspective on what's going on, if we hope to find a way to move forward as constructively as possible.

Education

For me, the top priority is education, and here I mean education at several different levels. In my comments I'm going to talk about some different types of approaches to education. Some of what we need to do is to *unlearn* some of what we think we already know. Education is not always about learning something new. Sometimes it requires us to *unlearn* in order to understand something in a different kind of way.

There is also education in the form of developing better, more accurate, more coherent frameworks for understanding what is going on, even as we are participating in the events around us.

There is a most urgent need to educate ourselves about Islam because it is the world's second largest religion. There is a great deal going on in various places where Muslims are the dominant majority, and much of that scene is characterized by unrest and disagreement among Muslims themselves. Many people today in the West, certainly in North America—political and religious leaders especially, I find—want to frame the current situation in the world and our immediate future in terms of what is called a "clash of civilizations." In my view, and this is one example of the unlearning, I want to suggest that perspective is both inaccurate and dangerous. It is simply not a helpful way to understand the dynamics of what is going on. In 1993, in *Foreign Affairs Magazine*, Samuel Huntington wrote an article "Clash of Civilizations?" in which he argued that world politics were entering a new phase. Three years later, he turned that article into a book titled *Clash of Civilizations*, this time without the question mark. It seems he'd answered the question for himself in those three years—that we are indeed immersed in a clash of civilizations. Huntington (1996) argued that the principal clash was between Western and non-Western societies, with a great deal of his focus centered on Islam. Fundamentally, what we now have in this argument is a recycled version of the Cold War thesis, one that now posits that the future conflict will not be so much economic and social as it will be ideological, with Islam and perhaps China as ascendant world forces, forces that are already threatening the West.

Huntington concludes his book with a survey describing what the West must do to keep our opponents divided. The West, he argued, must exploit differences and conflicts among Islamic states, while at the same time strengthening international interests and involvements that reflect and legitimate Western interests and values. He argues, that is, for an aggressively interventionist, even chauvinistic approach to much of the world. However, I think that the appropriate and more important approach should be one that sees the need to *understand* the changing world scene and the ways in which we can move forward toward reconciliation and cooperation among different cultures and different traditions. Why? Because we are all interdependent. By contrast, the conflict-of-civilizations mindset promotes a warlike approach and a mode of domination, one that advocates the West as the force that should dominate everybody else.

Interestingly, this idea of civilization and conflict predates Huntington. It took flight with Huntington, but the first person to speak in these terms was Bernard Lewis (1990) who is very widely read in the West. In an article in *The Atlantic Monthly* titled, "The Roots of Muslim Rage," Lewis, one of the influential voices that the U.S. government listened to in its preparation for the war in Iraq, stated:

> It should by now be clear that we are facing a mood and movement far transcending the level of issues and policies of the governments that pursue them. This is no less than a clash of civilizations—the perhaps irrational but surely historic reaction of an ancient rival against our Judeo-Christian heritage and the secular present; and the worldwide expansion of both. It is crucially important that we on our side should not be provoked into an equally historic but also equally irrational reaction against that rival (59).

Understanding Islam

My friend, the late Edward Said of Columbia University, noted a fundamental flaw with this whole approach of using sweeping generalizations about 1.4 billion Muslims scattered over five continents, with dozens of languages, traditions and histories. Both Lewis and Huntington present Islam or Muslims as somehow all uniformly enraged, as if 1.4 billion people were really only one person, and as if Western civilization is itself no more complex than a simple declarative sentence, and as if you can set up this kind of us-versus-them dichotomy that only fuels the notion of a clash of civilizations. Do you see my point? Many people sometimes embrace this attitude without even knowing what they're saying. Using this kind of duality and its simplistic terminology puts forward a notion that somehow civilizations are homogeneous and monolithic. They're not.

It is imperative that we see the deep anti-Islamic bias at work here. The idea that anti-Westernism is what defines Islam is highly suspect, and yet people like Lewis and Huntington promote the simplistic notion that Islam is somehow anti-Western and anti-U.S. It's as if all Muslims sit around all day and try to figure what to blow up next, as though that's their life's agenda. Lewis's premises are that Islam never modernized itself, never distinguished in any way between religion and the state, and that Islam is incapable of understanding other civilizations. If you know much about the history of Islam, all of that is just patently untrue. On October 17, 2006, *The New York Times* published a very interesting piece, "Can You Tell a Sunni from a Shia?" which claimed that most of the leaders, at least in the United States, four years into the war in Iraq, had not a clue about what the differences were between Sunnis and Shias, and that this included people on the intelligence committees who are supposedly being briefed all the time. The level of ignorance was astounding. But if you knew anything at all about Islam, you would know that long before Marco Polo and other European travelers, the Arabs had already been travelling throughout the east and throughout Africa, and that it was Muslims who, over many centuries, discovered and incorporated much from other civilizations.

More than that, Muslims have themselves contributed enormously to Western civilization as we know it. Indeed, our Western civilization is very much a product of Judeo-Christian-Islamic heritage, along with Greek and other influences woven in. Islam, we need reminding, is a very big part of that. When Europe was languishing in the dark ages for centuries, the Muslims led the world as a most advanced and sophisticated civilization, to which we can trace many of our disciplines. It wasn't necessarily that they invented all these things, as they did algebra, but that they incorporated developed and nurtured them, e.g., medicine, philosophy. Learning has generally been very important within Islam. One of the famous sayings attributed to Mohammed is that "you should seek knowledge wherever you may find it, even unto China." Muslims are not anti-intellectual by definition. On the contrary, if you know much about the history of mathematics or medicine or navigation or horticulture, then you know that Islam contributed significantly to these disciplines and introduced many of them. Much of what we know about Greek philosophy was lost in the West after 529 A.D., and was reintroduced to the west by Muslim philosophers in Spain. Some of our great thinkers of the Middle Ages and Europe e.g., St. Albert the Great, St. Thomas Aquinas, were deeply indebted to, and openly acknowledged the contributions of, their Islamic counterparts.

One of my favourite examples is a man named al Biruni (973-1048), a scholar, philosopher, mathematician who lived in what would be Pakistan today. The author of over 100 works, al Biruni made a number of impressive experiments, involving the observation of eclipses and sophisticated mathematical formulas, in which he determined both the curvature of the earth, and its radius and circumference (to within 200 km by today's measurements). All this centuries before Columbus!

We need to remember, too, that our university system was also influenced by Muslim learning centers. I attended Harvard, the oldest university in the United States. I was impressed when I got to Harvard and learned that it was founded in 1636. (I'm from Oklahoma which wasn't even a state until 1907.) Harvard was founded three centuries after

Oxford and Cambridge, and they, in turn, about four centuries after the Muslims had already established their own university system. Our use of the term "chair," I believe, derives from the early Islamic universities. The professor is the person who sits in the chair, while the students gather around his feet. Our learning histories, therefore, are so intertwined and so much more connected than most people imagine that this idea that Islam is anti-intellectual is simply unsupportable. This kind of misconception flourishes or is widely embraced only when people know very little about Islam.

Recently I spoke at a major conference in Texas and made the outrageous declaration that Jews, Christians and Muslims all perceive themselves to be following the God of Abraham. It's not really a terribly complicated or outrageous comment, but in Texas apparently it is; and so I'm being denounced left and right, defended left and right; and I've also been receiving letters from all over the world thanking me for my courageous stand in stating the obvious. Others ask: "How can you possibly call yourself a minister?" To know anything about Islam, however, is to know that my statement is not controversial at all. There are 15-17 million indigenous Arabic-speaking Christians in the Middle East who pray to "Allah" because they speak Arabic, and "Allah" is the Arabic word for "God." If you speak French it's "Dieu," At one level, then, it's no more complicated than that. At the same time, however, these traditions that all see themselves connected to Abraham also have different ways of understandings what we mean by "God." That's true among Christians and Jews and Muslims, but it's hardly a shocking revelation.

In May of 2007, the famous American evangelical pastor, Jerry Falwell, died. Sadly, he was a master when it came to misleading people about Islam. He would say such things as "Allah is not the same God as the God in the Bible," and "We're not talking about that same God." This is just another way of dismissing and writing off 1.4 billion people. The argument often has been that if you don't include the divinity of Jesus in your understanding of God, then you're not talking about the same God. To which I respond: Then Jews and Christians aren't talking about the same God either. At that point the conversation's meaning also changes because obviously Jews and Christians *are* talking about the same God, but, again, we don't have the same understandings. Pick any group of people and you will find a diversity of views about the ineffable reality we call "God." How, indeed, can we ever understand and define the divine reality with anything approaching certainty?

Looking for a Template

Religion and politics are linked, and education is the key to understanding this linkage. Currently, what is happening is that a number of groups, both in the United States but also in different parts of the Islamic world, are advocating particular visions of what it means to be a Christian-American and what it means to be an Islamic state respectively. Such people seem to believe that they have a template that can be known and followed. What I wish to argue is this: From our knowledge of the history of religious traditions, we can see that religion and politics have been linked in *various* ways, but that there is no fixed template for what that linkage looks like or what it should look like. We need to increase our awareness of how flexible this linkage has been throughout history. Let me give you brief examples from all three Abrahamic religions.

The Jewish State Template

The first thing we need to recognize is that Israel is the only state in the world today that describes itself as a *Jewish* state. Historically, what was the Jewish template and how did it emerge? If you read the Hebrew bible, you could argue that the vision is one that began with Saul, David and Solomon. The nation really begins to become a nation when the people of Israel cry out to the High Priest Samuel "Give us a king!" Samuel thinks it's a bad idea, and God Himself isn't so sure either; but eventually God says O.K. and Saul becomes the first king. That didn't turn out too well. Then come David and Solomon, and one could argue that their reigns are the pinnacle of Israel's history in terms of power and influence. The problems that follow along with the whole prophetic ministry are connected to how Israel lost its way, and to how the "nation" lost its connectedness with its moral foundations—after which there is a return to God and to the faith. Then the Jews are dispersed, and, lacking in any real sense of power, the image of nationhood is lost for a long time, When the Jews finally regroup and came back together, they formed an explicitly Jewish state, one that was to be a homeland and a safe haven for Jews. The Jews weren't then saying: "Well, let's go back and revisit the Samuel deal, and see if we can reconstitute what God wants us to do." No, they had already carved out something very different.

Within Israel today, what you find are very different visions about what defines a Jewish state. Indeed, how can a state be Jewish and, at the same time, democratic when a third to a fourth of the population is non-Jewish? These issues add to the dilemmas that Israel has faced over the years, particularly during its occupation, over the last 40 years, of the West Bank and Gaza; and they have been exacerbated.

The Christian Template

When we turn to the New Testament, the first words that probably come to your mind are Jesus saying "Render unto Caesar the things that are Caesar's and to God the things that are God's." (Matthew 22, 20-21) This statement somehow suggests that it is possible to separate these two realms. We also have the words of Paul urging us to "pray for those in authority over you" (1 Timothy 2, 1-3). People sometimes like to quote that, and pray for those in authority. Then they'll make a quick reverse decision such as: "Well, looks like God made a mistake with this one!" or "God couldn't possibly have wanted this person in power," and so Paul's suggestion doesn't always seem to hold up very well.

The Muslim Template

For Islam, as well as for Christianity, some form of monarchy or dynastic rule has been the dominant form of government. Along with it there is also the deeply entrenched mindset that Islam is a complete, seamless way of life in which religion, politics, economics, the military, the social—everything—are all rolled into one.

That, I say, is the enduring image, the enduring idea, but it is hard to find examples in Islamic history where that kind of seamless fusion was ever achieved in any visible, workable kind of way. You find a lot of debates going on within Islam today, about the illegitimacy of various governments. Right in the heart of Islam—Mecca and Medina—what kind of government do you have? You have a monarchy which is one of the very things that Osama Bin Laden and others rail against. How can this be called "Islamic"? They do, indeed, have a point; and yet this power structure has been a form of Islamic government throughout the centuries as well.

My point is that you can try to develop a template, but when you actually see what Muslims have done and what the Christians have done, you will find they have done all kinds of things, and that generally they have been experimental in adapting to circumstances. Some things, of course, worked better than others, and both cultures are still in the process of changing, defining and refining themselves. Now, with the advent of democracy or, as I prefer to say, with the advent of participatory government, we have an increasingly important component in the mix.

Democracy can mean so many different things, yet people use the term as though they know exactly what it means even though it covers different forms of participatory government in different places.

Looking Forward

Looking forward, I believe that we are in for a rough time. The next 10 or 20 years will be the most difficult. There are no easy answers or simple solutions, but I do think that there are positive ways to move forward constructively toward a more healthy and hopeful future. The road, I've already suggested, begins with education at several different levels: notably, defining our terms; developing better frameworks for understanding; developing an awareness and appreciation of the fact that part of what we're going to see and experience in our cultures may only be tentative and experimental. Future efforts will involve finding ways to combine religion, politics, and democratic principles in different structures. We see some of this explicitly in the Islamic world today. There are about 53 countries today with Muslim majorities, over half of which have some form of democratic process at work. One of the challenges is that the affirmation of democratic principles and procedures has sometimes been followed by a condemnation of countries when they go and vote for the wrong people. Democracy, we seem to think, is a good thing as long as the kind of people are elected that we in United States want to be elected. Democracy is great for the Palestinians, unless you vote for Hamas. When that happens, it's unacceptable, and so we're cutting off the money.

We see these socio-political experiments everywhere, and we need to appreciate that there is no one simple solution. If Muslims from the 53 countries, just average persons in those countries, were asked "Do you think that Islam can provide some kind of government structure that incorporates Islam in a meaningful way in the 21st century?" my guess would be that the large majority of them would say "Yes, I believe that's possible. I believe that's what we should do because Islam is our way of life, and it should shape and guide our government."

Even so, Muslims themselves differ widely in trying to make sense of all of this. Pakistan was founded as an Islamic state, and it's been a very difficult experiment for a number of decades. I know of nobody lining up to take classes from the Pakistanis on how to organize an Islamic state, and yet that was explicitly what they said they wanted it to be. The Taliban is an extreme manifestation of a vision of an Islamic state, and at the time of September 11, 2001, only three Islamic countries recognized the Taliban as legitimate: Saudi Arabia, the United Arab Emirates, and Pakistan. Most Muslims thought these people were crazy, and that this was certainly not the way they wanted to organize their states. These "little details" seem to slip by most Americans (I'm not sure about Canadians). This kind of limited understanding combined with a fear that all Muslims are bent on destruction makes for skewed perceptions.

In a book I'm now working on, Iran figures fairly prominently because I really believe Iran holds some of the best hope for the future. Since the revolution of 1979, Iranians have been engaged in a process of democratization. It has had to confront many problems, and while it's not a pure democracy—one might wonder just what that looks like—it has engaged in the messy business of electing people and implementing democratic structures. Look at what the Iranians did as part of its revolution: Despite all the negative images that many Westerners have, Iran did not hearken back to Mecca and Medina, and then form a government modeled on that view. Rather, while drawing from Islamic principles in many different ways, they borrowed heavily from Western parliamentary democracy. They now have a parliament, cabinet officials and a supreme court system; and they elect their President. None of that came out of Islam. Rather, much of this Iranian government structure is modeled on Western parliamentary democracy. People tend to forget this. I single out Iran because it represents one kind of experiment, one that has to cope with a lot of difficulties, and yet continues to struggle. Iran has endured, and I believe it holds out real hope as others look at ways to move forward.

The Example of Pope John Paul II

What is clear to me is that, in the 21st century, narrow sectarian forms of Christian, Muslim or even Jewish states are one-way, dead-end roads to disaster. What we desperately need are new approaches to interfaith understanding and cooperation that recognize several realities: that we are interdependent; that we live in the midst of pluralism and diversity; that there have to be ways to draw upon the best of our religious traditions but which, at the same time, affirm the values of diversity and respect both globally and locally. I believe John Paul II understood this and modeled something of this spirit throughout his remarkable tenure as Pope over three decades. In 1985, for instance, John Paul II addressed 80,000 Muslims at a football stadium in Casablanca. Listen to his words. "We believe in the same God. The one God, the living God who created the world. In a world which desires unity and peace but experiences a thousand tensions and conflicts, should not believers come together? Dialogue between Christians and Muslims is today more urgent than ever....Too often in the past we have opposed each other in polemics and wars." He concluded by saying: "I believe that God is inviting us to change old practices. We must learn to respect each other. We must learn to stimulate each other in good works on the path to righteousness." (John Paul II, 1985).

In 1986, John Paul II invited leaders from all the major religious traditions and many other religious traditions to Assisi for a day of prayer and dialogue. He was, I believe, the first Pope to visit a Mosque in Egypt and Damascus, and to visit a synagogue in Rome and then later travel to Jerusalem to meet with Jewish, Christian and Muslim communities. I believe, too, that John Paul II realized that traditional ways of thinking about God and others outside our own religious communities of faith were no longer adequate. Narrow thinking that fails to see that there is, in the end, really only one community, the human community, is theologically suspect and increasingly dangerous in our interdependent, 21st century world. In addition to education at many levels, we can and should also look for ways to model this future that we want and need.

A great deal has already happened, a great deal is happening, a great deal more needs to happen. Dialogue can work for us at different levels, and so it's important to pursue it vigorously at many different levels. We don't have to reinvent the wheel here. The Catholic Church and various Protestant Churches have been involved in this enterprise for some time, and we have wonderful resources available: on-line communication, pamphlets, booklets, the long experience of learning how some things work better than others. We have all kinds of resources to facilitate a program of intentional dialogue in our *local* congregations, and this I think is an increasingly important part of the overall educational process, and an important way of connecting people in our own communities.

Working Together

In addition to dialogue, I think it's very important that people of different religious traditions look for ways to work together on common concerns. To do that we don't have to be in theological agreement on the divinity of Jesus. In fact, we do this all the time right now. Consider the world of business for just one day and you will see it throughout the global economy. The most fundamentalist Christian is not going to bat an eye about doing business in Saudi Arabia. He's going to seize the opportunity, he's not going to be worried about whether his Arab counterpart believes in Jesus because economically we are all interconnected and interdependent. It would never occur to a Muslim, Christian or Hindu doctor, or to a research physician working on AIDS or cancer, to look at each other and say "We really can't work together on this problem of AIDS because we just don't have the same views about Jesus." We would be horrified if somebody did something like that. Of course, we bring who we are to the process, and it may be that we do so out of our faith and religious commitment, but we don't disqualify one another simply because of our religious affiliations. AIDS and cancer are problems that affect all human beings, and we bring the best we can bring to reduce their incidence. If a Hindu doctor discovers the cure, so much the better since we all gain.

We need to be doing things such as this, with the full power of intention unimpeded by sectarian differences. Building Habitat for Humanity houses might serve as both our motto and our inspiration. Whenever a Jewish and Christian community or a Mosque and a church pair together and build a Habitat house, I believe that two things happen in the process: the builders contribute to the common good of people who need that help and, at the same time, they have put into practice a theology of religious pluralism, something that I think is far more helpful than anything handed down by a member of the hierarchy in a remote office. We grow into a lot of our theological understanding through real-world encounters. So *be intentional,* but *do something constructive* in the process.

There are ways that we can live, and I would even say to model, this sort of commitment. I believe that the U.S. and Canada are the two countries that have the most hope of modeling something for the rest of the world when it comes to interfaith understanding and cooperation. We've now been engaged in a lengthy experiment; both of our countries have incorporated within our very fabric a significant degree of diversity as evidenced by our inclusion of Muslims, Hindus, Jews and Buddhists and many others. We don't see that same sort of incorporation in some of the European countries, and this is proving to be very problematic and will continue to become even more problematic.

The education level of the average Muslim in the United States is higher than the average level across the rest of the country. We need to continue to work seriously for this kind of result, to recognize that we have something that works, and with firm intention to nurture this kind of development. Education at various levels, dialogue, looking for ways to work together such as Habitat housing, cooperation in prison ministries—these are the kinds of undertakings in which we all share common concerns.

In Chapter Five of the Koran, there is a wonderful passage. I may be the only Baptist minister on the planet who periodically quotes what it says about religious diversity. It says: "If God had so willed, God would have created you one community, but God has not done so in order that God may test you. Therefore, compete with one another in good works. To God you will all return, and God will tell you the truth about that which you have been disputing." I think this is a wonderful image for all of us to have. It not only affirms religious diversity, it also affirms it as somehow being a part of God's plan. It urges us to compete with one another in good works: Be the best Christian, be the best Muslim, be the best Hindu...be the best whatever you can be. Let your competition be in the area of good works, and God will one day sort out the differences which we have been disputing. In the final analysis, we can leave the resolution of our differences to God. I think John Paul II understood and embodies this point, and so must we.

When it comes to religious and cultural differences, there are no easy answers or simple solutions. I don't have any magic formula to offer, but I think the way forward will become clear if we're willing to do hard work in the area of education, dialogue, cooperation, and if we stay open to experiments in religion, politics, pluralism, and cooperation. Some of these moves will happen in the next 10 years, and, as always, they will be the most difficult.

References

Huntington, S. (1996). *The clash of civilizations and the remaking of world order.* New York: Simon & Schuster.

John Paul II. (1985). Address of his Holiness John Paul II to young Muslims in Morocco. http://www.vatican.va/holyfather/johnpaulii/speeches/1985/august/doc uments/hf jp ii spe 19850819giovanni-stadio-casablancaen.html

Lewis, B. (1990). The roots of Muslim rage. *The Atlanic Monthly*, September, 47-60.

PART I

RELIGION AND THE PUBLIC FORUM

Introduction

If asked to identify the features that help to define *culture*, we would probably have no hesitation in adding religion to the mix. But when faced with the task of situating the place of religion within *society* or within the *nation*, the challenge is more daunting. Does religion—more precisely religious belief, structures and practices—have any place in the public sector, or should the state separate its functions (law, education, taxation, social policy) from any religious influence? Some insist that the public square should be "naked of religion," others seem quite willing to move into what many fear would be "a kind of religious terrorism."

The two chapters in this section deal with place of religion in society, and the tensions arising therefrom. In both Canada and U.S., religious belief and practice are constitutionally guaranteed freedoms. The presence of God has even been formalized in American currency ("In God we trust") and in our Commonwealth anthems ("God save the Queen," "God keep our land glorious and free"). However, while we can easily glimpse the presence of religious concepts and influences in public life, we do not, as in theocratic societies, have religious structures embedded in the governing apparatus. So far in Canada, we have resisted the inclusion of *sharia* in our legal sector.

Tensions are bound to emerge. What Moira McQueen calls an "aggressive secularism," that opposes the presence of any religious influence in the public, has emerged, and this translates even deeper into an active opposition to the expression of religious viewpoints in the development of law and public policy. Flashpoints are easy to recognize: morning school prayer; nativity scenes in public buildings; same-sex marriage; euthanasia; state supported abortion; public funding for selected religious schools in Ontario and Quebec; in Quebec, the introduction of an Ethics and Religious Culture course into all schools without parents' consent. Most recently, in both Canada and the U.S., the issue of polygamy, allegedly a divinely sanctioned practice, has become an embarrassment to governments, and a headline issue. And yet, because religion remains an inescapable fact of life in most democracies, it seems impractical, "unreasonable" to insist upon a *total* separation of church from state.

A deeper theme runs below the surface: Can there even be such a thing as a value-free society, since so much of our moral and social values system is rooted in religion and its history. Historically, our legal system drew from church or canon law, and ultimately from the Stoic notion of "natural law" (*ius naturae*), a foundational concept that affirms the values of reason and human life, the common good and religion. Indeed, the unavoidability of ethical discourse reveals itself in our everyday appeals to "justice," and when, in the debate over euthanasia, both sides invoke the language of "compassion" and "dignity." McQueen sees something "clearly dangerous" in the attempt to silence religious voices.

Given the wide sweep of information-media, Carol Stanton points out that there is even a question about what nowadays constitutes the "public square," and where we might draw the line. As part of that new defining, she sees a need to improve the understanding between believers and non-believers, and to establish what religion can best do in the public sector. What kinds of conversation would be necessary for religion to claim a rightful and useful place in society? Who are the parties to that conversation? Will the imperative to converse require as well a "mediating language," a willingness to bridge epistemological and moral diversity, indeed the very ability itself to listen? Following suggestions by Cardinal Ratzinger, Stanton asks what kinds of limits to religion and reason are involved. Is the community of believers prepared to confront its own pathologies? Is there even such a thing as a "cultural ministry" in which religion can contribute both to society and to its own re-formation? Indeed, what would such a ministry or *diakonia* look like?

The chapters by McQueen and Stanton comprise a lively challenge to the entrenched dogma of "the separation of church and state" because they show us that its unquestioned acceptance threatens to weaken our social and political fabric. At the same time, if we want to preserve a place for religion within the public square, we need to ask, and find answers to, some daunting questions.

CHAPTER ONE

RELIGION, LAW AND POLITICS

MOIRA MCQUEEN

Challenges to Religious Freedom

In a speech given by Cardinal Francis George of Chicago at the Library of Congress in February, 2007, he stated:

> It seems a battle has arisen between our older notion of a civic pluralism accommodating the religious beliefs of the vast majority of Americans on the one hand and, on the other hand, an aggressive secularism that seems quite intent on eliminating any religiously motivated idea, speech or action in civic and intellectual life (George 2007).

This sums up well the state of affairs in other Western democracies where, until now, the type of pluralism that the Cardinal describes has been well established. Those who think that religion has no place in the public sector have challenged the right of religious believers to make their views known. This is happening in many countries, including Canada. Some examples are as follows:

1. The British decision that Catholic adoption agencies must allow adoptions by same-sex couples, despite negotiations between the church and the government (Government of United Kingdom, 2006). Freedom of religion and its practical consequences, not just individual religious beliefs, but those as well of the official Roman Catholic Church, have been trumped by a decision that favours homosexual rights.

2. A report that Archbishop Angelo Bagnasco of Genoa received an envelope containing a bullet and a message with the star-shaped symbol of an Italian terrorist group, after he spoke out against government proposals to introduce legal rights for same-sex couples (Weston 2007.) Bagnasco had warned that if criteria for laws are reduced to a mere question of public opinion, then there would be no basis for rejecting calls to allow incest, or to ban political parties such as the recently proposed party for pedophiles in the Netherlands.

These comments were based on actual cases before the courts in Germany and the USA, and are not just speculation.

3. In Canada, the question of refusing public funding for religious schools continues to be raised. Recently, the *Literary Review of Canada* contained an article titled, "Whose Values Shall Prevail?" by political scientist, Professor Janice Gross Stein (2006), Chair of the Munk Center for International Affairs at the University of Toronto, dealing with this issue. Professor Stein suggested that the Catholic Church and other religions that do not follow so-called "Canadian values," should lose their charitable tax status, which would cause immense problems. In terms of the Canadian Charter of Rights, she suggests that the Courts would be the arbiters of values, and the arbiter of who complies with them. Other groups are also lobbying to remove separate funding for Catholic schools, and there will be some sort of alliance to bring this about.

4. The imposition of an Ethics and Religious Education curriculum in Quebec has resulted in the Quebec Bishops accusing the Quebec government of totalitarianism in imposing this curriculum without the parents' consent (Ouellet 2007). The chair of a working group on "The Place of Religion at School" had condemned the bishops' leader, Cardinal Marc Ouellet, for his negative judgment of the political process, a process which the chair sees as democratic, since the curriculum talks of seven or eight different religions (Proulx 1999). Cardinal Ouellet, for his part, noted that the section on Christianity does not even distinguish between Catholicism and Protestantism, a peculiar omission in a province whose heritage is so strongly French Catholic, despite the process of secularization. The Cardinal suggests that parents should be able to withdraw from this mandatory program and put their children into classes which reflect their choice of religion. As it is, 80% of parents already choose the option of Catholic moral and religious teaching available in Quebec public primary schools, so what is the rationale for moving to a universal curriculum?

Freedom of Religion as a Democratic Value

Those who think religious values should be promoted and protected remind us that freedom of religious expression is, and has been for a long time, a core value in democratic countries. So too are the efforts to protect individual conscience, especially in the workforce. The protection of these principles is a foundational value in any democratic state, in order to preserve human freedom in all its manifestations, including its spiritual and religious dimensions. At the same time, the idea of "the common good" is a time-tested hallmark in any society, especially in a democratic society, where people learn to respect differences, and to live together despite these differences as long as everyone's fundamental rights are observed.

How, then, can a society call itself democratic, pluralistic and, in Canada, multicultural, yet move towards excluding certain defensible views from the democratic political process? This is a point resting on logic and reasoning, one that everyone should be able to reflect upon, and is not just something based simply on religious belief.

Secular Values are not "Neutral"

Those who would try to completely separate religion from law and public policy claim that their judgments are "value free." This, however, is not very compelling. It is not really possible for anyone to be "value free." The very act of claiming to be so is in itself a moral stance; that is, a moral choice as to what values will be selected in public policy. Some claim that their choices are free from religious bias or influence. They forget or do not recognize that, as Pope Benedict XVI frequently reminds us, most western democracies are the cultural and historic heirs of the Christian tradition. Our legal systems reflect that morality and thinking to a significant degree since, whether we like it or not, our rule of law owes more to canon law and natural law theory than many people realize.

Democratic systems have built their legal systems largely around a notion of justice founded on equality, with human rights as a given of our common humanity or, more simply, of our very existence. Yet some modern laws have abrogated those rights, removing the basis of the right to existence from some who already exist, as in the case of abortion, and according that right to someone else. Those who do so may claim that they are free of religious values, but what are we to make of the value system they now apply to justify those claims? Those value systems may be utilitarian, consequentialist, relativist, or any combination of *isms*, but are they not similarly open to critique?

For some to say that their views are secular, as somehow implying freedom from compulsion or bias, or perhaps as implying that they are more rational or more sophisticated, is inadequate for purposes of moral debate. On the contrary, these values, assumed or invoked, are an expression of their underlying beliefs about the meaning of human life and how it should be treated, including the decision that it is right to exclude some views from the public arena simply because they are based on religion. This is a retrograde step in moral discourse in which one side decides that the other should not participate simply because the latter may have religious principles—as if that charge automatically precludes the possibility of those principles being reasonable.

The Use and Meaning of Language in Ethical Discourse

The moral language used in the legal and political arenas needs to be clarified. An example of this need can be found in current movements to legalize euthanasia, where both sides of the debate invoke the same terminology. Both claim "compassion" and "dignity" as key value terms. How do we sort this out? On the side of those supporting euthanasia, for example, one groups calls itself "Dying with Dignity." That title might make people think that the deliberate ending of life is more in keeping with human nature than natural death. What it more likely means is "death under my own control," which may or may not be dignified, depending on the circumstances.

Those who support living until the time of natural death also use the term "dignity." The deeper meaning here is that we now value and respect the human person at *every* stage of the journey, and at every stage of the disease which is threatening life. The person's life retains as much value up to the natural end, and is of so much worth that, while striving to relieve suffering, nothing should ever be done to hasten death. Suffering and death are not enemies to be avoided by deliberate termination of life, but are part of the continuing mystery of human life—an acknowledgment that there is more to us, more to the ultimate meaning of life and death, than controlling the time of our demise.

The other term widely invoked by each side is "compassion." Those who favor euthanasia say that compassion means supporting the person in bringing life to an end and avoiding actual or even future suffering. Euthanasia used to be commonly known as "mercy killing," and this notion also implies the same thing: that compassion in these circumstances means ending life. The suffering is eliminated because the person is eliminated.

On the other hand, those who respect life until natural death take to heart the more literal meaning of "compassion," "to suffer with," and this is what they know they must do. If a person is suffering, then to be compassionate means to be in active solidarity with that person's pain, to be doing all one can to support that person physically, morally and spiritually—to support the whole person, in recognition of that person's supreme worth and value. Suffering and death are seen to have a deeper human meaning, and the goal is to help the person live until he or she dies, as meaningfully as possible. A climate that encourages this level of meaning is possible, and it is one advocated by a Christian approach to life which calls upon its members to love their neighbours. This approach does not see artificially accelerated death as a benefit to the person, but rather sees the person's dying as an opportunity for human solidarity, or even growth—for Christians, a time of grace—as others help to maintain the person's dignity.

The difficulties involved at the level of language and meaning, therefore, are important aspects of the public debate, and so there is an urgent educational task for those who appreciate what is at stake here. People may be easily swayed by any procedure that claims to be dignified and compassionate, but we need to be clear what these words ("dignity," "compassion") mean with respect to their consequences for those who are ill, and with respect to their use in framing legislation.

Education on Ethical, Legal and Political Issues

The education task mentioned above has been taken up by many, and recently by the Ontario Conference of Catholic Bishops (2007), which has just issued a document titled: "Let Us Go to the House of the Father." The bishops thought that it was timely to give some instruction to their people about the Catholic Church's teaching on euthanasia, in light of the probability of new legislation to legalize it. The document is a teaching document, and is not directed against any particular political party or stance, but is meant to clarify what Catholics should take into consideration should new legislation arise.

Many people think the church should not be involved in politics, but this is unreasonable, demanding an unrealistic separation of church and state. In fact, the main arguments used by the bishops against euthanasia are based on natural law, and are not only specifically religious arguments which could be dismissed by non-believers. Natural law arguments are those conclusions based on our reasoning skills to work things out, and in which we draw upon both wisdom and experience. They are not arguments based on particular religious tenets. As rationally formulated arguments, they do not require scriptural reference to validate them, although the combined power of the two dimensions—natural reason and religious sources—can be compelling.

The Ontario Bishops' Conference statement reminds us that euthanasia and physician-assisted suicide are never allowed since they violate the commonly accepted prohibition against taking innocent human life. They remind us, as well, that it is important to understand that as long as nothing is done with the deliberate intention of causing death, we are not required to prolong life at all costs if the means of doing so are judged to be unduly burdensome or no longer effective. In cases where pain is great, it is permissible to administer pain relief even though such means may have the secondary but unintended effect of hastening the end of life. The Ontario bishops go on to urge Catholics to familiarize themselves with the relevant moral issues, and to prepare themselves accordingly. They appeal to physicians to obey the ancient medical injunction: "First, do no harm." They remind us that patients place their trust in the medical profession, and that legalizing euthanasia would undermine that trust.

Finally, the bishops conclude by talking about people's civic responsibilities, adding that Catholics have a right and duty to participate in the political processes of our democracy. They point out that the right to life and the care of the sick are not merely partisan issues, nor are they exclusively religious. The right to life is a fundamental human right, *the* fundamental right, and that protecting it no more depends on solely religious arguments than do our laws against theft, fraud or assault.

Because of this approach, the Ontario Conference of Catholic Bishops is able to communicate with other denominations and, indeed, with people of no religious affiliation. Their points, based on natural law and appeal to reason, are understandable by everyone, even if not always accepted by them.

At about the same time, the Catholic bishops of Scotland used the same approach recently when, on the eve of local elections, they published a letter inviting all Catholics "to look beyond the superficially attractive and fashionable to recognize those policies and values which are most in tune with the dignity of the human person and with the common good of our society" (The Bishops' Conference of Scotland, 2007). The wording is sensitive to the need to appeal to the common good as applicable to everyone in society, not just to Catholics, and is therefore neither exclusively "Catholic"—a contradiction in terms—nor dogmatically grounded. Who could reasonably object to that?

Freedom to Express Reasonable Views

Those who continue to insist that religious views have no place in law or politics seem to forget that it is membership in society that gives people a voice, and not adherence to a particular position, religious or secular. As the bishops' documents make clear, if an argument is reasonable, it deserves to be heard and taken into account. Excluding some voices simply because they are religious ultimately works against society and the common good, inasmuch as any social policy, if it seeks to be a just one, should be mindful of all relevant, reasonable arguments. Otherwise dictatorship of the secular mindset threatens to prevail, one that could exclude views which did not conform to its own standards (or lack of them, if relativism were to hold sway). Such a dictatorship would be antithetical to democracy, pluralism and the spirit of tolerance.

Religious bodies, therefore, must continue to promote their values as they always have done in a free society, with the aim of persuading secular society of their moral worth. The present trend of attempting to silence religious voices, and of discouraging them from taking stands on political issues, is dangerous. If that trend gains ground, then instead of working toward the common good, society may well settle for an ethic of individualism and relativism; and, in the absence of adequate moral standards, situations of discord and social chaos may emerge. It is unlikely that society could flourish in such a climate.

Conclusion

So far, under the Charter of Rights, the Canadian legal system has protected religious freedom of expression. It will be interesting to see how these rights are balanced against rights affirmed or protected in other parts of the Charter, for example those rights as they are invoked in the debate over same-sex marriage. As long as freedom of expression is guaranteed, however, every citizen is entitled to express his or her views in the business of shaping social values and in promoting the common good. Democratic freedom is ample enough to embrace the value of religious views, just as it does reasonable secular views, in shaping law and sustaining political life. To exclude either the religious or secular dimension could very well tilt us in the direction of an unjust society instead of inclining us toward the common good. If both religious and secular views are *reasonable,* we have good reason to expect that there will be a good deal of agreement between them.

In conclusion, then, I suggest that both religious and secular viewpoints are essential for the functioning of a reasonable, civilized society. Hopefully, if both are respected and maintained, the future of both society and religion will be less endangered than now sometimes appears.

References

The Bishops' Conference of Scotland. (2007). Pre-election pastoral letter, Eastertide, April 15

George, Cardinal Francis. (2007, February 13). At Library of Congress, Cardinal warns against secularism's dangers. Retrieved from http://www.catholicnews.com/data/stories/cns/0700915

Government of the United Kingdom. (2006). Equality Act, Part 3. Retrieved from http://www.opsi.gov.uk/acts/acts2006/pdf/ukpga_20060003_en.pdf

Ontario Conference of Catholic Bishops. (2007). Let us go to the house of the Father. Ottawa, ON: CCCB. April.

Ouellet, Cardinal Marc. (2007). La liberté réligieuse à l'école. Conférence de presse du Comité Action-Parents, March. Retrieved from http://eglisecatholiquedequebec.org/documents/pdf/20070312_l_ecole_et_la_liberte_religieuse.pdf

Proulx, J. P. (Ed.) (1999). Task force on the place of religion in Québec. *Religious education in the schools: A new perspective for Quebec.* Retrieved from http://www.meq.gouv.qc.ca/REFORME/religion/html-ang/ang/index.htm

Stein. J. G. (2006). Living better multi-culturally: Whose values should prevail? *Literary Review of Canada,* Fall.

Weston, J. (2007). Pope and Italian President give public backing to bishop threatened over opposition to homosexuality. Retrieved from http://www.lifesite.net/ldn/2007/may/07050106.html

CHAPTER TWO

NEITHER NAKED NOR SACRED: RELIGION IN THE PUBLIC SQUARE

CAROL STANTON

In the United States we have a built-in tension: We see ourselves as a religious people; yet, because of our congenital pluralism—our founding ideal of religious liberty—we also want to protect the freedom of those who are religiously unaffiliated.

This is not a new thought. The tension of holding these two ideals together, however, is being stretched to the breaking point. We struggle with a terrorism identified in many U.S. minds with religious fanaticism and politically connected to an increasingly unpopular war. We struggle, too, with immigration issues in which some churches are taking radical stands based on conscience while other churches judge those stands as flying in the face of the law. Continually, in our "melting pot," we are confronting the edgy issues of difference and belonging. Whether with the face of gender, race, country of origin, political partisanship or socio-economic status, these issues are stretching the fabric within our society and within our churches, synagogues and mosques.

The issue of the role of religion in U.S. society is played out against understandings and misunderstandings of the First Amendment and the separation of church and state, about which I cannot go into in depth here but wish to acknowledge. There are on-going constitutional questions, especially concerning issues such as the rules surrounding religious, tax-exemption status and access to federal monies.

A recent *New York Times* Sunday edition carried a piece about the Congressional grants known as "earmarks." A record 180 million earmark dollars were granted to religious institutions during the 108th Congress, which sat from 2003-2005. Federal regulations require that these monies be used for "non-religious" purposes, but the line is often blurred. Earmark grants to religious institutions have, in some cases, been successfully challenged by constitutional lawyers. Beyond the constitutional risk, there are other risks for faith communities, such as possible moral conflicts if earmark grants are attached to unacceptable appropriation items. There is also the risk of having one's moral voice muffled, that age-old problem of sitting down to sup with powers and kings.

Over the years in the U.S., we have bent ourselves every which way to make it work, relying on what Rousseau identified as a "civil religion" and Franklin called a "public religion." Yet, our "In God we trust" God tends to be borne out of a national definition and experience of ourselves as a generically Christian country rather than out of the experiences of particular faith communities. A recent *Pew Forum on Religion and Public Life* found that U.S. Americans continue to view their country as a Christian nation and are more supportive of religion's role in public life than they were in the 1960s, (The Pew Research Center for the People & the Press and The Pew Forum on Religion and Public Life, *Religion and Public Life Survey*, July, 2006). In an earlier (2002) Pew Survey, a majority of Americans supported religious pluralism, believing that a person can be a good American even if she or he does not have religious faith. However, by more than 3:1, they rejected the idea of churches and other houses of worship endorsing political candidates, and significant numbers said they would not vote for a well-qualified Muslim or atheist (The Pew Research Center for the People & the Press and The Pew Forum on Religion and Public Life, *Americans Struggle with Religion's Role at Home and Abroad*, March 2002, 3). Reverend Al Sharpton recently commented in public that he would not vote for Mitt Romney because, in his opinion, Romney doesn't really believe in God because he is a Mormon. Romney's answer was that the American people think it is important that candidates have a faith but they are not particular about *what* faith. That may or may not be true.

For the past 50 years, the U.S. Census has not asked for religious affiliation; therefore, those statistics must come from self-identification surveys. Recent information indicates that while 76% of the U.S. Population identifies itself as Christian, there is a growth rate in Christianity of only 5%. Those who identify themselves with Islam are only .5% of the U.S. population but have a growth rate of 109%; the growth rate for Buddhists is 170% and for Hindus, 237% (Retrieved from adherents.com, ARIS study, *Twenty Largest Religions in the U.S.*, 2001).

The face of U.S. religious pluralism is changing. Some argue that, for the sake of today's pluralism, all faith traditions should be privatized, and that the "public square" should be naked of religion. In reaction, others have entered the U.S. public square wielding a notion of the "sacred" which has, at its most extreme, taken the form of a kind of Christian terrorism. Public debate, hijacked by the attendant ideologies of partisan politics, is too often marked by incivility, epitomized by the preponderance of radio and television talk-show hosts who don't so much talk as scream—as if both they and we were deaf—and whose ultimate power is to shout down or cut off dissenting views. Jon Meacham, the Managing Editor of *Newsweek* magazine, maintains that both the right and the left in the U.S. feel they are losing, and that "this is a recipe for extremism and not particularly well-thought-out-debate" (Meacham 2006).

There is something else that is changing and it is captured in this question: *Where* do we locate the public square today? Some think of the public square as a literal space, defined by boundary and contour—a town square or hall, Tiananmen Square, the Washington, D.C. Mall, or any public street used by citizens for protest or support of issues. Since the 1950s we have had the electronic hearth of broadcasting—a social communication vehicle which went beyond print media in its power to bring us to a real-time, common awareness of *event*, such as the 1969 moon landing or, more recently, 9/11. As a result of our journey from tubes to chips, we have arrived at digital communication and a proliferation of information sources resulting in both a fragmentation of information and the formation of a new dimension for public debate, free of traditional time and space constraints.

As of March 31, 2007, the *Pew Internet and American Life Project* reports that of the North American population of almost 335 million, 70%, or 233 million, are on the internet. For a global perspective: Asia has almost 400 million users; Europe, 315 million; Latin America, 96 million; Africa, 33 million; the Middle East, 19 million and Australia and Oceania, 18 million. This does not include the use of iPods and other types of MP3 players, or the ubiquitous cell phones with their capability for text-messaging.

There have been concerns that the Internet would be harmful to democratic deliberation. Early research indicates that Americans on the Internet hear more points of view regarding candidates and key issues than other citizens. Internet groups such as *Moveon.org* entered the political arena in an unprecedented way during the 2004 election, and were able to mobilize thousands of people and dollars to promote its agenda issues. Now, a candidate without an interactive website is at a distinct disadvantage.

Here are some of the other negative predictions I have heard: People have increased stress due to being in a state of continuous partial attention; multi-tasking becomes a way of life; a whole generation will be unable to effectively read, write, think or work; the notion of presence is radically changed in the sense that we may be present-while-absent and absent-while-present. There are also positive predictions: People are less *audience* and more *co-creators* of information; there may come a time when we have global voting on some issues; at the very least, local conversations will be impacted by global conversations, and both local and global society will be changed in the process. Perhaps, most intriguing of all is the future possibility of a kind of "digital immortality" due to the possibility of downloading our brains, saving the activity, and, as it were, retrieving ourselves at will.

Communication media have become critical to the possibility of public debate and decision-making. In the United States, in the past, we depended upon the three major television networks and Public Broadcasting for our source of information and debate; now, we have hundreds, even thousands, of sources of information and places for discussion. As we move away from the networks, we leave behind the editors and gatekeepers of the past and inherit new filters. While discussion feels more democratic, in its purest sense, it is also more fragmented. For politicians and non-profit interests alike, the task of putting a message out into the public arena is daunting; for the individual, the level of personal responsibility for sifting and contextualizing information is enormous. We are only beginning to develop new "literacy" tools.

When we consider "Religion in the Public Square," then, from the reality of communication and information media, we must acknowledge that the public square of forty, ten or even five years ago is not the public square of today; and today's public square is not tomorrow's. If the respected theologian Walter Ong, S.J., is correct, our changing communication technology is not only altering the way we perceive the public square, it is also affecting our consciousness, the very *way* we think and perceive (Ong 1988).

With this background on the changing face of religious pluralism in the United States and the evolution of new ways of being public, I want to offer my thoughts in three areas: 1) an argument for why religion should not be privatized or become quiet in the U.S. public square, *especially* in today's shifting pluralistic society; 2) some new understandings that believers and unbelievers will have to hold if religion is to be public; and, 3) a proposal for a model for a "best public praxis," if you will, for religion in the public arena, a model which could lead to the reshaping of both religion and society. My own context is as a citizen of the United States and as a practicing Roman Catholic Christian. However, I hope my thoughts are broad enough to apply in some way to other pluralistic societies and to faith communities other than my own.

1) Why Religion Should not be Private Especially in Today's Pluralistic Society.

I will address this issue from two perspectives. The first perspective is from outside the religious context, from the view of a particular critical theory; the second perspective is from within a religious context, that of a Christian theology.

A Perspective Outside the Religious Context, From Critical Theory

One of the pleasures of studying a living theorist is observing the development of his thinking over the years. This is so with Jürgen Habermas, the German critical theorist. I wish to be clear that I do not approach Habermas's work uncritically. There are lacunae in his thought which I have analyzed in a longer critique drawing from both media studies and from theology. What I want to offer are a few of his insights which, in my opinion, retain validity today. I also want to show how over time, in his thinking, he has brought religion from the private into the public realm.

Habermas is known primarily for his major works, *The Structural Transformation of the Public Sphere* (Habermas 1989) and his two-volume, *The Theory of Communicative Action* (Habermas 1984, 1987). His interest has been the possibility of reasoning people to debate and make decisions about issues affecting their lives, in the process creating a social space between the privacy of the life-world and the state, which he calls the *public sphere*. In *Structural Transformation* he charts the rise of a particular historical public sphere, and, among other things, traces the role of the press and publicity, pointing out the distortions and manipulations that can occur in the formation of public opinion. In *The Theory of Communicative Action*, Habermas builds his theoretical case for the emancipatory possibilities of non-coerced, authentic communicative action in a constitutional democracy. His concern is for a healthy public sphere. He notes that when systems which depend upon instrumental rationalities, such as power and the economy, permeate the life-world, which depends on rationalities of understanding and inter-subjectivity, then the social space of the public arena becomes colonized and shrinks. One example for Habermas is the over-commercialization of the mass media, leading not to the healthy public sphere it was meant to form, but to its obstruction. It makes a difference whether citizens are viewed primarily as *consumers* or as *publics*, especially when a society is engaged in public debate on issues affecting the life-world of its citizens. He also expresses concern about the effect of spin on the formation of public opinion through public discourse. This concern found a current voice in the media aftermath of British Prime Minister Tony Blair's resignation. Critics were reported to have decried Blair's era of spin, saying it had "rotted discourse" (Dowd 2007).

Until recently, Habermas left no room for religion in his theory of the public domain, either from a philosophical or social scientific point of view. For him, religious traditions were too particular to be universalized. People come to consensus through the force of the most persuasive argument, not the force of tradition. Also, in his theory of communicative rationality there are only three validity claims in modernity—truth, rightness and authenticity. He argued that religious traditions and their theologies look for ultimate validation somewhere outside of the dynamic of communicative rationality, and so could not be tested by it.

In 1989, Habermas held his first public discourse with theologians, initiated by the University of Chicago Divinity School. During this conference, theologian Francis Schlusser-Fiorenza criticized Habermas for a failure to trace the critical development of religion in modernity. At conference end, Habermas admitted, as a social scientist, that the "critical appropriation of the contents of religious tradition" was ongoing (Browning and Fiorenza, 237). He also admitted that he had too hastily agreed with the Weberian thesis that once religious world views had collapsed, all that could be salvaged from religion was some kind of universalized ethical system. He said:

> Religion...which has been largely deprived of its world-view function in society was still indispensable in ordinary life for normalizing intercourse with the extraordinary. For this reason...philosophy, even in its post-metaphysical form, will neither be able to replace nor repress religion as long as religious language eludes....translation into a discourse that gives reasons for its positions (Browning and Fiorenza, 237).

More recently, in *Between Facts and Norms* (Habermas 1996), Habermas locates religion in the non-governmental and non-economic network of associations emerging from the private sphere, comprised of citizens who are looking for meaningful interpretations of their lives and who want to influence the public opinion and decision-making institutions of their own society. They do this by moving issues from the periphery to the center.

In 2006, Habermas and then-Cardinal Joseph Ratzinger, now Pope Benedict XVI, held a public conversation entitled, "The pre-political foundations of a democratic constitutional state." At issue: What holds us together, reason or religion? The exchange resulted in a little book with the title, *The Dialectics of Secularization: On Reason and Religion* (Habermas & Ratzinger 2006).

Here is a much too brief synopsis of this exchange. Habermas's position is that in the face of a globalizing world and global world markets, the social solidarity of the self-legitimized constitutional state is not always holding. Citizens who are meant to be active participants in democracy, exercising their rights both for their individual interests and for the common good, are becoming de-politicized and apathetic in the face of overwhelming forces. The public sphere is shrinking. In addition, the history of world failures, horrors and injustices leads to profound fragmentation and disappointment, and a deep scepticism that any world governmental body would be able to provide the glue necessary to hold the world together. Here, again, Habermas returns to his earlier themes, pointing to the penetration of the global market forces and rationalities into all aspects of the life of citizens.

In the end, Habermas suggests two things: First, Western philosophy, due to the co-penetration of Christianity and Greek metaphysics, still holds genuinely Christian ideas, conceptual clusters with a heavy weight of meaning, such as, *responsibility, autonomy, justification, history, remembering, new beginning, innovation, emancipation, embodiment, individuality, fellowship.* He says philosophy transformed these terms without emptying them. For instance, "man in the image of God" translated into "the identical dignity of all men that deserves unconditional respect." This goes beyond the borders of one particular religious fellowship, makes the substance of biblical concepts accessible to a general public, and also includes those who have other faiths and those who have none. He suggests that philosophy and religion can and must learn from one another, since they have shared roots.

The second part of Habermas's diagnosis is that the balance achieved in the modern period between the three great media of societal integration is now at risk. This is because the markets and the power of the bureaucracy are expelling social solidarity (understood as a coordination of action based on values, norms and a vocabulary intended to promote mutual understanding) from more and more spheres of life. He suggests that it is in the interest of the constitutional state to deal carefully with *all the cultural sources* that nourish its citizens' consciousness of norms and their solidarity. This awareness, which has become conservative, is reflected in the phrase "post-secular society." This term, he says, does more than give public recognition to religious fellowships in view of the functional contribution they make to the reproduction of motivations and attitudes that are socially desirable. It also reflects a normative insight that has consequences for the political dealings of unbelieving citizens with believing citizens. There is an increasing consensus that certain phases of the "modernization of the public consciousness" involve the assimilation and the reflexive transformation of both religious and secular mentalities. If both sides agree to understand the secularization of society as a complementary learning process, they will also have cognitive reasons to take seriously each other's contributions to controversial subjects in the public debate.

In his own contribution to the question of what holds us together in a free state, Cardinal Ratzinger acknowledges the pathologies of religion, and points out that reason has presented the world with equally dangerous pathologies. He sees the need to set limits on both religion and reason, and says that both need to publicly acknowledge their mutual dependence. He adds that, in the world of today, this public acknowledgement must be done in an intercultural context, in which both Christian faith and Western secular rationality must learn to listen and accept a genuine relatedness to other cultures, so that any Euro-centrism or Western hubris may be avoided, and so that a "universal process of purifications" can proceed.

A Perspective From Within a Religious Context, Catholic Christian Theology

I turn now to a more theologically-based argument for why religion should not be privatized in today's pluralistic society. In her book, *A History of God* (1993), Karen Armstrong suggests that a concern for the here and now, concrete action in the world, goes back to the roots of monotheistic religions. Alienation from the world is a constant temptation for religions which stress belief in a heaven or paradise hereafter. This type of alienation can make believers passive in the face of the challenges of their present existence.

At the heart of its orthodoxy and orthopraxis, Christianity has a public mission and an incarnational grounding. The universal and non-discriminatory largeness of the Gospel, the good news of the risen Lord, have, from the beginning of Christianity, been the foundation for the Christian community's world mission. Theologian Ben Meyer finds this in earliest Christianity, where Christological reflection provided both the source of identity (as a principle of unity) and self-definition (as a principle of diversity) (Meyer 1986).

This public mission of the Church was interpreted variously through history, and distortions of it often led to violence. In the Roman Catholic Church, it was not until Vatican II that the Church began to develop formally a public theology that embraced the modern world and sought ways to engage creatively with it. Documents such as *Inter mirifica (The Decree on the Means of Social Communication)*; *Unitatis redintegratio (The Decree on Ecumenism)*; *Nostra aetate (The Declaration on the Relation of the Church to non-Christian Religions)*; and *Dignitatis humanae (The Declaration on Religious Liberty)* (Flannery [Ed.] 2004), all reflected a Church more willing to dialogue and engage with others and the "otherness" of modern society. In other words, the Church was to open itself to self-critique as well as to the critique of others.

Until the time another Council is called, Catholic Christians remain in a period of *reception* of Vatican Council II. This is an important point to consider. For over 40 years we have been drawing interpretations from its documents while often forgetting that we remain in a period of active reception.

Vatican II had three, interrelated guiding principles. One was *ressourcement*; the second was *aggiornamento*; the third was *unity*. The first, *ressourcement*, involves the Church listening to its own tradition, going back to its biblical, patristic and liturgical roots to find resources for reflection. The second, *aggiornamento*, "throws open the windows," in the words of Pope John XXIII, who had called the Council into being. The Pope was convinced of the goodness of the world and was calling the Church to read the "signs of the times," to listen to the social sciences and other churches, and to be open to the new questions presenting themselves. He firmly believed that the old truths always needed to find new expression if the Church was to fulfill its universal mission. The third guiding principle, *unity*, captures the ecumenical intent of the Pope, his call to a new unity in Christianity, partly in order to engage more authentically with other faith communities. Since Vatican II, this call to be public has a formally recognized ecumenical and interfaith dimension.

Since Vatican II, the work that has been done on the development of a public theology in the United States makes a distinction between *privatization* and *secularization*. Theologians Michael J. Himes and Kenneth R. Himes maintain that restricting religious faith to the category of the individual deprives both the individual and society of the integrating force of religion. Religious concerns may be had and religious convictions held, but if privatized they do not impact other dimensions of a person's existence. Though the Himeses acknowledge that the impulse to privatize religion is a by-product of secularization, they maintain that *secularization* (the removal of many aspects of life from religious control, as opposed to *secularism*) is a good thing and should not be resisted by religious believers. Secularization has forced Christianity to develop new ways of being engaged with society without seeking to control it. (Himes & Himes 1993)

It was precisely because of this paradigm shift within the Catholic Church's theology that Catholic theologian Francis Schussler-Fiorenza criticized Habermas for failing to trace the critical development of religion in modernity. Churches, says Schussler-Fiorenza, *are* communities of interpretation within those very networks that Habermas says constitute the life-world of citizens. Churches engaged in a continual self-critique and mutual critique provide an institutional locus in society, in the public, for discussion not only of questions of justice, but also of questions of the good, and the common good (Browning & Schussler-Fiorenza 1992).

2) Some New Understandings That Believers and Unbelievers Alike Must Come to if Religion is to be Public

At least three conversations need to be going on simultaneously in order to reach the new understandings we must have in society for religion to be a public force: an internal conversation within any given faith community; one between believers and believers; and, one between believers and unbelievers. Each conversation carries its particular challenge.

The Conversation Within a Faith Community

What has happened in the Roman Catholic faith community since Vatican II stands as an example of the conversation and conversion needed *within* a faith community. Pope John XXIII recognized the gap that existed between the church and contemporary life. Theologian David Tracy maintains:

> Every classic tradition, including every classic spiritual tradition, needs both retrieval and critique-suspicion…and…continuing conversation by the community constituted by its history of effects (Tracy 1977, 124).

The Council offered the church, which is always called to be *ecclesia semper reformanda*, new *historical*, *pastoral* and *ecumenical* frameworks for its theology, making it a less closed system and opening ecclesial space for the development of a public theology.

Within an *historical* framework, the role of the church's theology is immanent critique, employing a self-critical openness to its past history, abuses as well as contributions. In addition, theology is called to be open to other methods and critical theories which may help with the process of retrieval and the hermeneutic of suspicion. This dialogue enables a theology to respond to the new questions of an age while, at the same time, opening up its prophetic capabilities.

The *pastoral* framework of Vatican II helps the Church as institution to remain connected with the life-world of believers, the life-world which is integral for the communicative action Habermas sees as central for solidarity in society. This pastoral awareness also alerts theology to the need to take the experience of the faith community into consideration in its theologizing. Ecclesiologist Joseph Komonchak says theology's critical tools cannot be found in some realm divorced from the faithful's experience of the church. He writes: "When the Church is considered only in specifically theological terms, its relevance to the wider world of human experience is lost to view, and the privatizing tendencies of post-Enlightenment religion are encouraged" (Komonchak 1995, 12).

The failure of the U.S. Catholic Church to be pastoral in its clergy's sexual abuse crisis uncovered the serious pastoral disconnection operative in the past and continuing systemically into the present. Tracy's hermeneutic of suspicion is important because Christian self-understanding is not immune to the long-term distortion that is possible when biases are hidden. In 1976, in *Studies in Religion*, Jesuit theologian Bernard Lonergan wrote this chilling description:

> the shortcomings of individuals can become the accepted practice of the group; the accepted practice of the group can become the tradition accepted in good faith by succeeding generations; the evil can spread to debase and corrupt what is most vulnerable while it prostitutes to unworthy ends what otherwise is sound and sane (Lonergan 1976, 345).

Finally, that Catholic theology after Vatican II has an ecumenical framework implies a valuing of unity in diversity and pluralism. If this value is held up internally, within Christianity, then it is possible for it to extend to the quality of the Church's engagement with other faith traditions and within the public arena at large.

While Catholics do remain in a period of reception of Vatican II, this has not always been a smooth process. Internal disagreement and divisions within the Catholic Church over the past forty years have often obstructed the engagement with culture that Vatican II intended. Different interpretations of Council documents are sometimes used as "ammunition" for partisan-driven agenda and perhaps, as some have suggested, only a larger crisis of belief in society will draw the Catholic Church and other faith communities out of their self-absorption.

The Conversation Between Believers and Believers

A cultural crisis of belief and meaning is perhaps being felt more immediately in Europe than in the United States. The recent tug-of-war in the European Community (in which the Pope took part), over whether to include Christianity's contribution in describing the factors which make up the identity and culture of Europe, is witness to the reach of secularism. Yet European values studies have repeatedly confirmed that the young, especially, are identifying themselves as "religious" even though their attendance at religious services continues to drop. The English Dominican priest, Fr. Timothy Radcliffe, in a lecture at Westminster Cathedral in 2005, says Europe is now being described as "believing without belonging" (Radcliffe 2005).

The shared challenge for all faith communities and a topic for conversation among them is how to remain in contact with the millions who are looking for God—and for the good, the true and the beautiful—but not looking in the Church, synagogue or mosque. Radcliffe, speaking about the specific role of Christianity in Europe, says that Christians could bring peace to a warring, multi-religious Europe because they are able to understand, better than atheists, the role of faith and the importance of religious symbols in the lives of other believers. Would not this approach also apply to the virtues and values that authentic religious communities share in common, such as the belief in human dignity, compassion, common good and justice? There is the hurdle of difference to be gotten over first. It is important to remember that there can be a great deal of diversity within traditions as well as between them; there are different strands carrying the same name. Even the so-called Christian Right is not monolithic. Many evangelical Christians are disturbed by the anti-intellectualism and belittling labelling of extremists. This calls for another kind of conversation between believers. Chris Hedges's thesis in his book about the Christian Right says that these believers are the best ones to confront extremists within their own fold (Hedges 2007).

The challenge grows more complex when the confrontation is *between* faiths, and the conversation is attempted with the fanatical sector of a given faith. Fear becomes a partner in this conversation, and there is often pressure to hold fast to the hard-line for the sake of holding on to adherents. Again, this is a place for the moderates of a faith to come to the fore, to help with the understanding and conflict-resolution that must be a part of the conversation if it is ever to be held. While we always want to hold out for the *possibility* of dialogue, it may not always be *possible* to dialogue.

The Conversation Between Believers and Unbelievers

Richard John Neuhaus wrote that the "remedy for the naked public square is not naked religion in the public." He added, "...publicly assertive religious forces...will have to develop a mediating language by which ultimate truths can be related to the penultimate and pre-penultimate questions of political and legal contest" (Neuhaus 1987, 62).

In the conversation between Habermas and Ratzinger, Habermas made the point that the Christian concept of the dignity of every human person has translated into the universal, philosophical concept of human rights as enshrined in democratic societies.

In *Black Theology of Liberation* (1970), James Cone remarks that in the Civil Rights movement of the 1960s, Reverend Martin Luther King, Jr., took the Hebrew biblical tradition of justice and liberation and the democratic tradition of freedom, and joined them with the New Testament idea of love and suffering. In doing this, he was able to challenge all Americans to create the beloved community in which all are equal. The strategy was Ghandian non-violence; the influence was the Negro church.

In addition to this mediating or translation process around religious concepts and symbols, there is need for a certain degree of mutual literacy on the part of both believers and non-believers if they are to have fruitful conversation in the public arena. This very much speaks to the point both Ratzinger and Habermas make about the opportunity in a post-secular world for all worldviews to have space and mutual learning. This is especially relevant for the conversation between religion and science: Each must be at least knowledgeable about the language and terminology of the other, and hold a certain respect for the tradition of the other.

The responsibility for believers is to be intelligent and intelligible, civil in discourse and active listeners in dialogue—seeking agreement where possible, but mutual understanding always. The responsibility for unbelievers, as Habermas suggests, is to recognize in authentic faith-communities other legitimate, interpretive worldviews which have something to offer to the post-secular world.

The politics of a post-secular world have to face the full import of the valuing of diversity, including epistemological and moral diversity. As Stephen Carter writes in *The Culture of Disbelief*:

What is needed…is a willingness to listen, not because the speaker has the "right voice" but because the speaker has the "right to speak." Moreover, the willingness to listen must hold out the possibility that the speaker is saying something worth listening to; to do less is to trivialize the forces that shape the moral convictions of tens of millions of Americans (Carter 1994, 230-231).

3) A Model for Religion in the Public Square: *"Cultural Diakonia"*

The term *cultural diakonia* originates with Gotthard Füchs (Füchs 1988). The term is meant to refer not to an uncritical slavery to whatever a culture is purveying; rather, it refers to service to the deepest social space, the grounding place within a society for a healthy public sphere and for agenda-setting. *Cultural diakonia* is ministry to the shared common ground of the larger culture.

Churches are among those institutions in a society which help form personal identity as well as cultural meaning. In addition, faith communities encourage personal agency for the promotion of religious values such as justice, compassion and the common good, values often shared by those who are religiously unaffiliated. Through intentional *cultural diakonia*, churches are in a unique societal position to lend institutional infrastructure to actions which nurture a healthy public sphere and social agenda-setting by bringing peripheral issues to the center of power in civil society.

In the Roman Catholic Church, Vatican II re-aligned Christian Catholic theology with the historical consciousness necessary to address the new questions and needs within human society. The Council emphasized the sacredness of human persons and their freedoms and responsibilities for justice within their common life. This resonates with Habermas's thesis that the transforming capacity of communicative action, with its rationality of mutual understanding, contributes to a healthy public sphere.

What follows are several examples which, in my view, represent *cultural diakonia* in action.

Methodology of National Conferences of Catholic Bishops

In the 1980s, the United States Conference of Catholic Bishops (USCCB) employed a methodology of open consultation in writing their pastoral letter on nuclear war and deterrence, *The Challenge of Peace (1983)*, and their letter on the economy, *Economic Justice for All (1986)*.

They also utilized open consultation in an ultimately failed effort to write a pastoral letter on women.

In the first two instances, the bishops' committees invited involvement from within and without the U.S. Catholic Church in the drafting process. This unprecedented approach prompted discussion within a broad public, and also attracted the attention of the news media. In the case of the letters on peace and the economy, the results were documents which were more accessible in language, and more widely accepted and promoted than in the past.

The bishops adopted a similar methodology for the nine-year committee effort to write a pastoral on women. Seventy-thousand Catholic women across the United States participated in a series of consultative sessions held nationally and within dioceses. I was personally involved in the design and implementation of the Florida Diocese of Orlando's consultation which engaged 1200 women. In the end, the pastoral on women never saw birth. It was during this particular process that the Vatican intervened in what was properly a national conference's project. "Under pressure from the Vatican and some of its own members, in the late 1980s the bishops' conference abandoned the practice of open consultation" (Christiansen 2007, 2).

The Irish Catholic Bishops Conference used a similar methodology in the drafting of its initial guidelines on clergy sexual abuse: *Child Sexual Abuse: Framework for a Church Response* (Irish Catholic Bishops' Advisory Committee on Child Sexual Abuse, 1996). After convening and implementing a writing committee consisting of civil, medical and social experts as well as church hierarchy and spokespersons, the Irish bishops held listening sessions with a variety of relevant social-service agencies within the Republic of Ireland and Northern Ireland. They followed this up by sending an embargoed copy of the proposed guidelines to all relevant social-service agencies for early reading. The writing committee made it clear that this was a document in process and subject to change, thus sending the signal of welcoming input.

Because of their involvement in the process, by the time the bishops' committee held its first media conference announcing its publication, a level of acceptance already existed within the social-services public, a public whose response might have shut down the bishops' process. The release of the publication as a document subject to change allowed the issue to have breathing space in a society already reeling from the revelations of abuse by clergy. The Irish bishops, through their public action resulting from their own internal abuse crisis, alerted Irish society to the larger, shared problem of child abuse. This process constructively contributed to a deeper public discourse on the problem of sexual abuse in Irish society.

The consultative methodology used by both national bishops' conferences on issues of importance to the larger civil society, directly contributed to the quality of public discourse on those issues. Religious leaders in both countries entered the public discourse in a manner which respected the diversity of their pluralistic societies, while allowing them to contribute their insights and values to the public debate.

FOCUS—Federation of Congregations United to Serve

FOCUS is a federation of different religious congregations which unite in order to serve the needs of their larger community. A member of FOCUS in Central Florida described the organization as "a bridge between the people and officials. We don't do anything people can do for themselves; we empower them to take action" (Hughes 2006).

FOCUS polls people in order to identify their concerns. They take up the issue that tops the list for those living in a neighbourhood or area of a city. The interdenominational congregations involved use their infrastructures both to empower the people affected and to bring the social issue to the attention of those in authority. They have taken on such issues as the code enforcement on junk cars, insurance for children, crime, and a neighbourhood situation where older people were being terrorized by nightclub clientele.

The process FOCUS uses, of bringing an issue from the periphery to the center, is a good example of what Habermas described in *Between Facts and Norms* as a public, cultural role for faith-communities. The faith-communities involved in FOCUS have moved beyond their role of forming personal identity and providing cultural meaning for their own believers to the denominationally transcending role of joining together in order to exercise diaconal service to the public sphere. They do this by providing institutional infrastructure and the empowerment of personal agency to address real human needs within the larger, civil society.

The Independent Film, The Power of Forgiveness, by Martin Doblmeier/Journey Films

I have included the work of Doblmeier as an example of *cultural diakonia* largely because of the way the film-maker used his own creative process to prompt a broader, public discussion and awareness.

Doblmeier, a Catholic Christian, often uses the lens of his faith-tradition in making films. He noticed that the topic of forgiveness was one that was popping up in all areas of life—medicine, psychology, religion. He began gathering stories of forgiveness, and made a film that would eventually air on Public Broadcasting System (PBS).

As he worked, he began to realize that the United States was being shaped by war and revenge. He wanted to tell the stories of people who were finding other ways of responding. He found family members of those who died in 9/11. He found the families of victims and families of perpetrators who bonded together to educate children about the futility of crime. He interviewed members of the Amish community about the way they model forgiveness, and especially about their handling of the much publicized murder of some of their children in their own schoolroom.

Doblmeier took a rough cut of the film around the United States, asking only that an inter-faith audience be invited to view the cut, and then to discuss with him what they saw, what they were thinking. He showed the rough cut in almost 100 centers, colleges and churches. I was part of organizing a viewing in a parish in Winter Park, Florida. Six hundred people of all ages and religious traditions showed up to view and discuss the film.

Doblmeier's process is a one-person *cultural diakonia*. His own faith-tradition offers him a lens through which he does his independent film-making. But he breaks out of the "independent" role by taking the creative process out into the public arena for input and discussion, even before he has finalized it for PBS distribution. In this way, his work, *The Power of Forgiveness*, was a catalyst for a community-based discussion of one of the most pressing social issues in the post 9/11 world of the United States.

Conclusion

The tension we feel in the United States between our ideal of religious pluralism and its reality will undoubtedly remain, and it will undoubtedly become increasingly global. We sometimes wonder: Are there limits to inclusivity? As the world turns, people are killing one another because of their different worldviews. Often these worldviews include religious labels. In pluralistic societies, and even in growing democracies, religious leaders, for their part, have a choice to make: feeding into the diminishment of some or helping to liberate others by calling them to another way of being in the world. This alternative way of being in the world is one in which believers offer the best resources of their religious traditions—compassion, concern for the common good, a belief in the dignity of the human person—all this in order to help nourish vital and diverse public squares for the 21st century.

References

Armstrong, K. (1993). A *history of God*. New York: Vintage Press
Browning, D. S., and F. Schüssler-Fiorenza (Eds.). (1992). *Habermas, modernity, and public theology*. New York: Crossroad.
Cone, J.H. (1990). *Black theology of liberation*. Maryknoll, N.Y.: Orbis.
Carter, S. (1994). *The culture of disbelief*. Garden City: Anchor Press.
Christiansen, D., S.J., (2007). Of many things. *America*, 196:17.
Dowd, M. (2007). Labor's love lost. *The New York Times*, Op-Ed, Sunday, May 12, p.13.
Flannery, A. (Ed.). (2004). *The Vatican collection: Vatican Council II, Vol.1, The conciliar and post conciliar documents*. New York: Costello Publishing Co.
Füchs, G. (1988). Cultural diakonia. *Concilium: International Journal for Theology*, 1988: 4, (110-19,198).
Habermas, J. (1984). *The theory of communicative action*. Vol. I, *Reason and the rationalization of society*. T. McCarthy (Trans.). London: Heinemann.
—. (1987). *The theory of communicative action*. Vol. II, *Lifeworld and system: A critique of functionalist reason*. T. McCarthy (Trans.). Cambridge, MA: Polity Press.
—. (1989). *The structural transformation of the public sphere*. T. Burger and F. Lawrence (Trans.). Cambridge, MA: Polity Press.
Habermas, J., and J. Ratzinger. (2006). *The dialectics of secularization: On reason and religion*. (F. Schuller, Ed.; B. McNeil, Trans.). San Francisco: Ignatius Press.
Hedges, C. (2007). *American fascists: The Christian right and the war on America*. New York: Simon & Schuster.
Himes, M. J., and K. R.Himes. (1993). *Fullness of faith: The public significance of theology*. Mahwah, N.J: Paulist Press.
Hughes, Phoebe. (2006).Telephone interview by the author. October, 2006.
Komonchak, J.A. (1995). *Foundations in ecclesiology*. Boston, MA: Boston College.
Lonergan, B., S.J., (1985). The ongoing genesis of methods. In: F. Crowe (Ed.) *A third collection: Papers by Bernard Lonergan*, New York: Paulist Press and London: Geoffrey Chapman, (146-65). Originally

appeared in *Sciences religieuses/ Studies in Religion* 6 (1976-77), 341-55.
Meyer, B. F. (1986). *The early Christians, their world mission and self-discovery*. Wilmington, DE: Michael Glazier.
Meacham, J. (2006). The Christmas wars: Religion in the American public square, *Pew Forum on Religion and Public Life*, December 12.
National Conference of Catholic Bishops. (1983). *The challenge of peace: God's promise and our response.* Washington, D.C.: NCCB Publishing.
—. (1986). *Economic justice for all: Pastoral letter on Catholic social teaching and the U.S. economy*. Washington, D.C.: NCCB Publishing.
Neuhaus, R. J. (1987). Nihilism without the abyss: Law, rights and transcendent good. *Journal of Law and Religion* 53, 62. Reprinted in M.J. Perry, (1999) *Religion in politics: Constitutional and moral perspectives,* 78. New York: Oxford University Press.
Ong, W., S.J. (1988). *Orality and literacy: The technologizing of the word.* London & New York: Routledge.
Radcliffe, T., O.P. (2005). Christianity in Europe. *Faith in Europe: Westminster Cathedral Cardinal's Lecture Series*, May 2. Retrieved at www.columban.com
Tracy, D. (1997). Fragments and forms: Universality and particularity today. *The Church in Fragments: Towards What Kind of Unity?* G. Ruggieri, and M. Tomka (Eds.). *Concilium* 3: 122-129.

PART II

RELIGION AND SCIENCE

Introduction

For the last two centuries, the issue of science and religion has been on the table. Many have taken the view that science and religion are incompatible, that one must choose between them. Others have argued that they cannot be incompatible because ultimately both are of divine origin. A focal point in this debate has been the theory of evolution. Both papers in this section deal in some fashion with the topic of religion and science.

A prominent focal point for the clash between science and religion has been the theory of evolution set forth by Darwin in his *The Origin of Species* (1859). In his paper, "Darwinism vs. Intelligent Design, in a Religious Context," Hudecki argues that Darwinism was largely responsible for the tension between science and religion. In the 20th century, that theory was challenged by advocates of what has come to be called "Intelligent Design," the central proposition of which is that certain features of the universe and of living things are best explained by positing an intelligent cause.

In his paper, Hudecki critically examines the arguments and evidence supporting both Darwinism and Intelligent Design and argues that the intelligent design approach can defuse the tension between religion and science.

In his paper, "Science, Religion and the Illusion of Certainty," Lococo explores the paradox inherent in the pursuit of certainty and shows how it is that both science and religion present different ways of attempting to resolve the paradox. He argues that dialogue is essential as a generative middle ground and that the future of religion requires that we no longer fight the paradox but rather tap into the creative energy in the dialogue between science and religion.

The dialogue between science and religion is far from over. The debate about the meaning and implications of the theory of evolution will certainly continue to elicit responses from both sides, and the struggle to understand how science and religion relate to one another and to the broader human community will undoubtedly be an important issue for the 21st century.

CHAPTER THREE

DARWINISM VS. INTELLIGENT DESIGN IN A RELIGIOUS CONTEXT

DENNIS HUDECKI

Introduction

There is a tremendous debate going on in the intellectual world between Intelligent Design theory and Neo-Darwinism. Neo-Darwinism is the synthesis of classical Darwinism and modern genetics, and is also sometimes referred to as the "modern synthesis" or the "synthetic theory." In this paper, I will refer to Neo-Darwinism as "Darwinism." Intelligent Design questions Darwinism and proposes that science may have to recognize that at least some biological systems exhibit a kind of design that random natural causes cannot explain. It is my contention that the Intelligent Design movement is making a vital and critical contribution to questions regarding the origins of life. It is marshalling from a definite point of view a host of compelling objections, some new, some old, to Darwinism, on both the empirical and philosophical levels. Also, it has introduced an alternative, non-Darwinian template by which to observe biological phenomena—a template that invites serious consideration. Sociologically speaking, I recognize that Darwinism is as dominant as ever in the scientific community and that Intelligent Design is hardly on the scientific map. But I believe that Intelligent Design is raising serious intellectual issues that will have to be addressed in the future.

What makes debates about evolution so intense and ongoing has to do with the fact that the issue touches upon the existential realm. Theories about relativity or quantum mechanics are indeed engaging. But as soon as the evolutionist purports to describe where "we" come from—not just our bodies and our biology but the whole of the human self—the issue becomes existentially weighted, having implications about the human mind, if there is one, or the soul, if there is one. Thus Darwinism has been embroiled from the beginning in not just scientific debates, but also philosophical and theological ones.

Regarding this issue, Kierkegaard, who believes in the legitimacy of science and the scientific method, wrote in his journal in 1846 that most of what flourishes under the name of science in any given time is not real science but "curiosity." What passes for science, in many cases, Kierkegaard is saying, is a kind of shallow, but perhaps exciting, speculation that goes beyond what is warranted by the evidence. Let me continue to paraphrase his thought. This curiosity, according to Kierkegaard, becomes especially dangerous and pernicious when it would encroach also upon the sphere of the spirit and interfere with the ethical. For Kierkegaard, our lives ought to be based on qualitative decisions we make when we ask questions out of a profound and passionate sense of wonder. But according to Kierkegaard, science's tendency to claim to know more than it does about ultimate questions cheats people out of this sense of wonder and replaces it with a quantitative, ever-ongoing discourse that lacks decisiveness. Individual resoluteness is dissipated in the process (Kierkegaard 1941).

Yet, is it true that evolutionary theory infringes upon the world of spirit? Why cannot one simply adopt the Thomistic view that since true science can never be in conflict with true faith, the believer need not worry about what is happening in the world of science. According to this view, science attempts to answer empirical questions with its experimental methodology and is thereby limited by its methodology from addressing higher spiritual (or metaphysical) questions. Science deals with the efficient causes of things while philosophy and theology deal with final causes. Science cannot in principle, then, infringe upon the spiritual. The two are compatible and complement each other. For example, regarding evolution, a theist could say that it is possible that Darwinian evolution is true and that it might have been God's way of creating a diversity of species. In other words, evolution could be seen as part of God's design.

I do not think that this approach works, however. While it would be too strong to say that Darwinism is essentially tied to philosophical naturalism—the view that all explanations must be materialist and mechanistic—it is plainly true that Darwinism, like most or all other scientific theories, is a thoroughly naturalistic explanation for the development of life on this planet. Ernst Mayr—one of the most influential evolutionary biologists in the 20th century—I think overstates the case when he claims that Darwinism is a complete explanation, replacing divine intervention (Mayr 1982). Certainly, it seems beyond the reach of science to refute the idea of divine intervention. But the fact is that Darwinism strongly suggests to almost all of its interpreters that it has all the ingredients for a complete explanation of the biological development of life between the time that bacteria by themselves existed on this planet to the present. If God had an interventionist hand in the development of life, in certain instances, as many religious people believe, the Darwinian model would be false. The only room for God in Darwinian theory is at the beginning, where a deist-type, non-interventionist God could have arranged scientific laws to be such as to guarantee that humans would eventually be a product of natural, evolutionary forces.

But this idea of a purely natural, mechanistic explanation for the development of life creates another problem for religious belief (assuming that being forced into deism is already one problem). Many religious traditions believe that the Aristotelian cluster in humans of choice, morality, language and reason creates a quantum leap, so to speak, between humans and the animal world. There is no room for such a leap in Darwinism, however, since the theory is committed to evolutionary development by way of small, gradual steps. This being so, the tendency has been for evolutionists—or at least thinkers interpreting Darwinian evolution—to argue that there is no such quantum leap. The human being that emerges out of the Darwinian system, as interpreted by certain philosophers, is a biologically driven organism, not categorically different from an ape, say, or an elephant.

Now this kind of biological determinism may be true. From the beginning of Western philosophy, philosophers have been divided over what kind of being we are, whether or not we have a soul, whether or not we have free will and whether we are all that different, ultimately, from animals. I am arguing in this paper that one is not warranted in thinking that such issues have already been resolved by evolutionary theory.

Let me make one last introductory note. Many theologians see no problem with a materialistic, mechanistic universe and a purely biological conception of the human being. A huge topic in philosophy these days is whether it is possible to hold that mind, free will and consciousness, in the strong, traditional senses of these terms, can be explained in straight materialistic terms. Maybe they can. But once again I am arguing that that debate ought to be carried on in its own right, and that we ought not to bury certain options by prematurely conceding that biologism has been proven by Darwinian evolutionary theory. Let's now turn to the debate.

In what follows, I will begin by presenting the views of Darwin and Neo-Darwinism. I will then discuss a series of problems that are raised by Darwinian theory. I will first discuss the distinction between microevolution and macroevolution and consider to what extent, if any, the former is evidence for the latter. This requires a discussion of breeding, and its limits. Second, I will discuss whether genetic mutations can do all the evolutionary work that Darwinists say they can do. Third, I will briefly consider whether there has been enough time for evolution, under the Darwinist model. Fourth, I will discuss the extent to which the fossil evidence supports Darwinism. Having discussed these four issues, I will then end this chapter with a discussion of Intelligent Design theory, pointing out what I consider to be some of its more promising aspects.

Darwin and Neo-Darwinism

Darwin published *The Origin of Species* in 1859 and since then his work has been the dominant intellectual position regarding where life came from and the origin of species. In the century leading up to Darwin, scientists were successfully establishing the idea that organisms appeared on Earth in successive ways of increasing complexity and that, generally speaking, each new wave had many of the components of the wave that came before it as well as some new components. We now know for example that there are great biological similarities between, say, humans and chimpanzees, coyotes and wolves, moose and deer, and fir and pine trees. Thus, it has been fairly well established, and is not now a controversial issue, that for perhaps 3.5 to 4 billion years, life forms have multiplied and diversified and become more and more complex over time and that they can be grouped into classes that have similar internal biological structures.

The idea that more complex life evolved from less complex life has been a serious idea in the intellectual world since at least pre-Socratic times. Anaximander, for example, around 540 B.C.E., thought that humans and other land animals evolved from fish. What is distinctive about Darwin's position, however, is that he put forward a hypothesis that provides a purely naturalistic mechanism that would explain how one species evolved from another. When an organism reproduces, Darwin argues, one or more of its offspring might attain, due to inner variations, a characteristic that is new and different to that species. When this new offspring reproduces, it passes on this new characteristic. If this characteristic increases the survivability of that animal or plant, then it is more likely that the offspring having this new characteristic, and its offspring, will survive than the offspring that does not have this characteristic, given a scarcity of resources. Over time, this new and different characteristic will become a normal part of the species. Darwin called this process "natural selection" and soon afterwards others began to call it "survival of the fittest." Organisms that are the most fit will produce more organisms like themselves than organisms that are not as fit to survive. Gradually these kinds of changes occur over millions of years and their cumulative effect is what explains the tremendous diversity of life we now find on earth.

In the early part of the 20th century, modern genetics was then folded into Darwinism to add more detail to how the evolutionary mechanism works. This synthesis between genetics and Darwin (i.e., Neo-Darwinism) explains the random variations in terms of either random genetic mutations or built-in genetic variations that have randomly become selected. The former explanation—genetic mutations—has done the heavy lifting for Darwinians. Thus, over millions and millions of years, those mutations that turned out to be advantageous for survival, the theory runs, add trait after trait to a species and in doing so create new and more complex species.

Microevolution and Macroevolution

What evidence or arguments are there to support this theory? The first piece of evidence that a Darwinian will typically bring forth will be an example of adaptation or microevolution. These are some of the most popular examples: fruit flies and pepper moths adapting to different environments;[1] insects adapting to insecticides; HIV resistance to antiviral drugs; bacteria adapting to antibiotics; finches in the Galapagos adapting to the drought of 1977 by being able to adjust to bigger seeds; or the ability of sickle-cell anemia, a genetic mutation, to resist malaria.

This kind of microevolution, or adaptation, is accepted by almost all modern thinkers, biologists and non-biologists alike. Even in the human realm, it might be the case that skin colour, height and other physical traits differ from one group to another as these groups adapt to different environments.

The big question, though, is whether microevolution or adaptation proves what needs to be proved, namely that there could be so much change that new categories of species could evolve from old ones. Over time, for example, could fish evolve into amphibians and reptiles, reptiles evolve into birds and mammals, and humans evolve from an ancestor shared with the apes? In other words, could *microevolution* lead to *macroevolution*?

I think that the answer is that it could. There is no evidence, however, that it has. When everything is said and done, the examples that are put forth as evidence continue to be the very same organisms that they always were. Adaptation starts and ends with fruit flies, moths, bacteria, etc.

Thus adaptation does not itself explain how the moth became a moth, and the fruit fly a fruit fly.

Breeding and its Limits

Darwin had a different view of the powers of microevolution. For him, there was almost no limit to how a species could be changed. And one of his biggest arguments for this view consisted in his calling attention to the phenomenon of artificial selection—or breeding. He believes that his theory of great change through gradual variation is "not hypothetical." He writes:

> The great power of this principle of selection is not hypothetical. It is certain that several of our eminent breeders have, even within a single lifetime, modified to a large extent some breeds of cattle and sheep....Breeders habitually speak of an animal's organization as something *quite plastic, which they can model almost as they please*....Youatt, who was probably better acquainted with the works of agriculturalists than almost any other individual, and who was himself a very good judge of an animal, speaks of the principle of selection as 'that which enables the agriculturist, not only to modify the character of his flock, but to change it altogether. It *is the magician's wand,* by means of which he *may summon into life whatever form and mould he pleases'* (Darwin 1859, 30-31). (Emphasis mine.)

So for Darwin, as we see from the above quotation, an animal's organization is "something quite plastic." Breeding is a "magic wand" by which an agriculturist can completely change the character of an organism. The history of breeding animals and plants, however, indicates that there are definite limits to how much organisms can change. This history leads to conclusions that are exactly opposite to the ones that Darwin drew. Beginning in 1800, breeders sought to increase the sugar content in sugar beets. According to biologists Lester and Bohlin, the breeders, after 75 years, were able to raise the sugar content from 6% to 17%—but no further (Lester and Bohlin 1984, 95). Lester and Bohlin cite many other examples. Breeders can select for woolly sheep, for corn with more oil and protein, for faster and bigger horses, but they always reach limits. Tall humans can keep reproducing with tall humans but we never get 12 foot tall humans. We don't get, as Lester and Bohlin say, plums the size of peas or grapefruits, no matter how intense is the artificial selection process (Lester and Bohlin 1984, 96). Breeding has limits, and when taken too far tends to cause the organism to get weakened, deformed or sterile.

Consider studies of bacteria. They reproduce rapidly. Given scientific and technological advances in the laboratories, generation upon generation of bacteria can be produced in a very short order. Large populations can be reproduced, and large numbers of mutants can be observed. But, as Lester and Bohlin (1984, 88) report:

> Never has there arisen in a colony of bacteria a bacterium with a primitive nucleus. Never has a bacterium in a colony of bacteria been observed to make a simple multi-cellular formation.

As the French zoologist Pierre-Paul Grassé, (1977, 87) himself an ardent evolutionist, puts it:

> What's the use of their unceasing mutations if they do not change? In sum, the mutations of bacteria and viruses are merely hereditary fluctuations around a median position; a swing to the right, a swing to the left, but no final evolutionary affect.

Likewise, consider the fruit fly, Drosophilia. With a generation time of less than two weeks, several generations of it can be observed. Selective breeding can be used to try to make evolution happen. Yet, as Francis Hitching (1982) has famously said, the fruit fly just remains a fruit fly. Lack of change, or stasis, seems to be the rule. I will say more about that later.

Genetic Mutation as the Key Mechanism for Neo-Darwinism

Let's take a closer look at the genetic theory that Neo-Darwinism invokes. Although gene-pairs carry a great deal of variation within themselves, neo-Darwinists do not think that these variations could account for the unfolding diversity of life that we find on earth. It seems that the explanation must have something to do with genetic mutations. And one of the dominant theories of mutation has to do with gene duplication, due to copying errors in genetic replication. Because of a malfunction, a gene becomes suddenly duplicated. Now according to neo-Darwinists, the ancestral, original gene remains and carries out the functions it always has while the new gene is free to accumulate mutations that can eventually lead to new functions and possibly new organs (Lester and Bohlin 1984). This is the theory.

But the facts do not support the theory. What are usually presented as the best examples of evolution due to gene duplication are myoglobins and hemoglobins. These are complex blood molecules that at various times in the last 650 million years are said to have evolved into different chains, with different structures, ultimately arriving at the modern hemoglobin structure. The modern structure is tetrameric—more complex than the simple structure that existed at the beginning. This is perhaps the best example provided of what could be accomplished through gene duplication.

But what does this example show? After 650 million years of various duplications and mutations, the various genes involved have not changed their basic functions. They began, as Lester and Bohlin (1984) point out, as oxygen transporting genes and remain that way after 650 million years.

Furthermore, there is still not anything like conclusive evidence that even the change from the monomeric myoglobin to the modern tetrameric hemoglobin was brought about by gene duplication. Explanations are still in the realm of speculation.

A theoretical problem facing Neo-Darwinism in this regard is the fact that mutations almost always constitute a loss of information. There are some exceptions such as back mutations that activate genes that were previously disabled. But mostly, mutations constitute a loss. It is not out of the question, however, to hold that a loss of information could be beneficial, as is possibly the case of the flightless cormorant, found in the Galapagos Islands. Peter Scheele speculates that it perhaps had to focus on swimming and diving because it lost its ability to fly. It survived, Scheele speculates, due to its enhanced skills whereas other birds that could fly became extinct (Scheele 1997). Dr. Lee Spetner, a bio-physicist, argues that bacterial resistance to antibiotics is caused by a loss of genetic information (Spetner 1997). The bacterium, he argues, loses, by a genetic mutation, the specific site on which the antibiotic was designed to attach. Furthermore, he goes on to claim that there has yet to be one observed instance of a genetic mutation adding new information or new complexity to an organism (Spetner 1997). Dawkins (1997), a zoologist and one of the leading contemporary advocates of Darwinism, was once asked to give such an example, and he could not name one instance.[2] Yet, Darwinism takes as one of its foundational claims that the ever-increasing complexity of organisms over time is due to mutations.

The "Not Enough Time" Objection

If it is true that mutations almost always have a deleterious affect upon the organism, another problem emerges. Mathematicians since the 1960's have insisted that, given that there are perhaps 4 billion years to work with and that perhaps only .01 percent of mutations are beneficial, there is not even close to the amount of time for genetic mutations to cause the kind of diversity of life we find on earth. They calculate that the amount of time required would take billions of times longer than the 4 billion years life has existed on earth (Moorhead and Kaplan 1967).

The standard response to the "not-enough-time" objection is exemplified by some remarks made by Ernest Mayr who, as I already mentioned, is a leading figure in Darwinian theory. He says the following in response to the objection: "Somehow or other by adjusting those figures we will come out all right. We are comforted by the fact that evolution has occurred" (Mayr 1967, 30). I mention this response here to make a general point about the debate between evolutionists and their opponents, and as an introduction to the next part of my argument regarding the fossil evidence. Evolutionists most often talk as if they already knew that their theory is true. Evolution is a fact because microevolution or adaptation is a fact. So when an unsuspecting interlocutor raises objections like the ones I am raising, or like the ones I am going to raise regarding the fossil evidence, the response usually is along the lines of Mayr's. Typically, the response is that while evolution is known to be true, the detailed arguments have not been worked out yet. Findings that support evolution are celebrated, while counter-evidence is just seen as a problem needing to be solved and not something that casts any doubt on the theory.

The Fossil Evidence: Stasis and Sudden Appearance

From Darwin's time onwards, and it is still the case today, the fossil evidence is actually more of a problem for Darwinism than a help. The leading critics of Darwin, in Darwin's day, were palaeontologists and geologists. Darwin himself (1859,171) asked the question: "...Why, if species have descended from other species by fine gradations, do we not everywhere see innumerable transitional forms?" Why is it that what we see today are distinct species, clearly different than one another, and not a continuum? Darwin answered that the transitional groups, being less fit than the species that actually survived, die off quickly in the formation of what turns out to be the survival of the fittest. So it is not surprising that the transitionals are not with us today.

But what about the fossil record? Shouldn't the fossil record be teeming with transitional life forms, forming a gradual parade of forms from bacteria on up to elephants and humans? But such a continuum was also missing from the fossil record in Darwin's day. Darwin himself wrote that "the most obvious and gravest objection" that can be urged against his theory is the lack of fossil evidence, and it is for this reason, he says, that "all the most eminent paleontologists...and all our greatest geologists... have unanimously, often vehemently, maintained the immutability of species" (Darwin 1859, 310).

Of course, Darwin hoped that fossil evidence would be found in the future—especially now that scientists knew what to look for. But, arguably, the fossil evidence is still weak. Do we now, today, see evidence of a continual transition from one species to another? No. Steven Jay Gould, a leader among evolutionary theorists, puts it bluntly: The fossil evidence, far from painting a picture of continuous transitions, has instead painted entirely the opposite picture: In *The Panda's Thumb* he writes:

> The history of most fossil species includes two features particularly inconsistent with gradualism:
>
> (1) Stasis. Most species exhibit no directional change during their tenure on earth. They appear in the fossil record looking much the same as when they disappear. Morphological change is usually limited and directionless.
>
> (2) Sudden appearance. In any local area, a species does not arise gradually by the steady transformation of its ancestors; it appears all at once and "fully formed" (Gould 1980, 181-82).

As we will see below, these observations pushed Gould towards an attempt to revise classical Darwinian theory.

Regarding "stasis"—the relative unchangingness of species—Stephen Stanley (1981), another strong evolutionist, argues that in cases where we can observe species over long periods of time, what is usually observed is the fact that species undergo little or no change. He lists, for example, sea urchins and horseshoe crabs, each unchanged over 230 million years, bats, unchanged over 50 million years, sturgeon unchanged over 80 million years, and alligators unchanged over 35 million years. Regarding "sudden appearance," each of the examples I just mentioned appeared in a relatively sudden and finished way. The earliest horseshoe crab found in the fossil record is nearly identical to the horseshoe crab that exists today.

Perhaps the biggest fossil-related problem that faces Darwinism is what is called the "Cambrian Explosion." Regarding this phenomenon, Dawkins writes:

> The Cambrian strata of rocks...are the oldest ones in which we find most of the major invertebrate groups. And we find many of them in an advanced state of evolution, the very first time they appear. It is as though

they were just planted there, without any evolutionary history (Dawkins 1986, 229).

Before the Cambrian explosion, life was at a very primitive state consisting mostly of bacteria and algae. But suddenly, about 550 million years ago, there appeared some 5000 species. Most or all of the basic body-plans or phyla for animals appeared during this time. And there is hardly any fossil evidence leading up to the appearance of these groups.

Darwin knew this was a problem: He wrote of the Cambrian explosion that it may truly "be urged as a valid argument against" his theory (Darwin 1859, 308). The situation, though, may recently have gotten worse. A team of geologists (Bowring et al. 1993) concluded that the entire Cambrian explosion occurred within a five-to-ten-million year period—again, presenting, if the findings are true, a further problem for Darwinian theory. The new findings add even more support to the metaphor of a simultaneous "explosion" of life-forms rather than the slow, linear gradualism that Darwinian theory would predict.

If the evidence from palaeontology is so bad, why does Gould still support evolutionary theory and insist that the fossil record proves it? Gould and his colleague Nils Eldredge revised Darwinism to better reflect the fossil record, as they saw it. Their new theory, called "Punctuated Equilibrium," while holding fast to the Neo-Darwinian mechanisms of natural selection and genetic mutation, holds that changes occur very fast. These sudden changes occur when there are windows in the environment for rapid change, and when animal and plant populations are isolated from the normal gene flow that tends to hinder evolution. Furthermore, according to Stanley (1979), who also supports punctuated equilibrium, there could be some kinds of mutations "in regulatory genes" that while appearing fairly insignificant in the embryonic stage could have huge effects in the grown animal. Dawkins (1986, 235-36) speculates, for example, that one small mutation in a snake might lead to an extra "vertebra—which has to come in as a whole unit—and along with the extra vertebra all the extra skin, bones, blood tissues and muscles that go along with each vertebra." The trouble is, however, that there is no independent evidence to support these speculations. Furthermore, the theory is still reliant on genetic mutations as the mechanism for change—a mechanism that I have argued has serious theoretical problems.

Further Observations on the Fossil Evidence

Gould (1981) also thinks that some things found in the fossil record in fact constitute positive evidence for Darwinism. He makes a strong argument that there is fossil evidence for some intermediary links. Therapsids, a mammal-like reptile order, could possibly contain descendents for mammals, possessing as they do characteristics that are both reptilian and mammalian.[3] Gould also thinks that there are some reasonable candidates for a common ancestor from ape to human. Some apes may have walked upright. But these possible intermediates, which themselves are open to differing scientific interpretations, are rare exceptions to the general absence of possible intermediates between species.

Just a note on "hominids": Gould (1987, 64-70) mentions five human ancestors. But, as Phillip Johnson (1993, 82, n.2) argues, two seem clearly on the ape side and three are already fully human. A half-ape-half-human has yet to be found in the fossil record.

It should also be noted just how speculative a stage science is still at when it comes to evaluating fossils, including possible fossils pointing towards human ancestors. Nebraska Man, the key fossil of the Scopes trial in the 1920s, turned out to be a pig. Piltdown Man, which for 40 years was held up as key evidence for Darwinism, turned out to have been a fraud. Solly Zuckerman, an eminent scientist with a specialty in primates, and a strong Darwinist, compared physical anthropology to parapsychology and argued that the speculation in this field is so astonishing that it is legitimate to ask whether much science is to be found in this field at all (Zuckerman 1970). Colin Paterson, a highly respected evolutionist and senior palaeontologist at the British Museum of Natural History, regarding evidence for transitional forms, stated: "I will lay it on the line. There is not one such fossil for which one could make a watertight argument. The reason is that statements about ancestry and descent are not applicable in the fossil record" (Patterson 1979). And Stephen Stanley (1981, 95), who is, as mentioned earlier, a leading evolutionist, states "the fossil record does not convincingly document a single transition from one species to another."[4]

Summary of Problems Found in Darwinism

To sum up, the evidence for Darwinian-type of evolution seems thin. Its main argument is that since adaptation is a real phenomenon, so too must macroevolution be a real phenomenon. I have argued, however, that there is no strong evidence that microevolution leads to macroevolution. Second, genetic mutations are still not known for sure even to be the cause of adaptations or variations, since they almost always bring harm to the organism. Adaptations or microevolutions could simply be caused by inherent genetic variations that are already in the organism. Third, it has yet to be shown that genetic mutations can contribute to the building of new biologic structures or new major organs. Fourth, assuming that genetic mutations could cause macroevolution, there has not been enough time for that to happen. Fifth, the fossil record, with a few exceptions, leads to a picture quite different than the one that Darwinism would predict. Sixth, punctuated equilibrium, having no supporting evidence apart from the fossil record, is more of a description of how species appeared throughout history than a new explanation of how species were formed. Punctuated equilibrium is still burdened by the Neo-Darwinian theory that change occurs because of genetic mutations—a theory that I have argued is severely flawed.

Intelligent Design

Let's turn to Intelligent Design. Intelligent Design argues that some biological phenomena exhibit so much evidence of design that they could not have come about through random, mindless causes. Before looking at that argument, let me make two introductory points. First, it should be noted that Intelligent Design is different from creation science. Creation science starts with faith. It starts with the idea that the biblical God exists and that the account of creation in Genesis is literally true. It then tries to find scientific evidence to support its viewpoint. Intelligent Design, on the other hand, makes no religious assumptions. It holds that if there is some sort of God or higher intelligent force, questions regarding the existence of this God or this force, as well as what attributes it might have, are beyond the competence of science, given that such questions are not empirical in nature. Such questions are philosophical and theological, not scientific. Second, it should be noted that Intelligent Design does not rule out the possibility that natural selection can be used to explain large portions of biological development. Its claim is only that not all biological development can be explained in a Darwinian fashion.

The starting point of Intelligent Design, as Dembski points out, is that in some of the sciences, and in mathematics, there are well-developed theories for detecting the difference between design and randomness. Dembski mentions, for example, the SETI project (i.e., the Search for Extraterrestrial Intelligence) that looks for non-random sounds from outer space. In other words, it is looking for sounds that are the product of Intelligent Design. Also, archaeologists and anthropologists routinely have to decide whether something is natural object or a designed object (e.g., a tool or an artwork) Dembski then asks the question: "What if these techniques could be formalized and applied to biological systems, and what if they registered the presence of design? Herein lies the promise of intelligent design" (Dembski 2004, 311).

Two of the most interesting concepts to come out of the Intelligent Design movement are Dembski's notion of "specified complexity" and Behe's (2004) notion of "irreducible complexity." Dembski says that a million number sequence picked randomly is a complex sequence but not specified. On the other hand, if a sequence of a million numbers complied exactly with an independently specified sequence, than there is reason to believe that the sequence is not random but rather caused by design. Dembski is attempting to argue that the information sequences in the DNA molecule—the codes required to assemble the protein molecules in the right pattern along with its machines and other inner workings that allow it to survive—are not likely to have been produced by chance. The odds are too great. As it stands now, I think that Dembski's idea is a promising one, developing as it does the concept of "design" in a scientific context.

Behe's notion of irreducible complexity is likewise promising, and it is the concept that is currently getting the most attention. Behe (2004, 353) defines an irreducibly complex system in this way:

> I ...[define] an irreducibly complex system as: a single system that is necessarily composed of several well-matched, interacting parts that contribute to the basic function, and where the removal of any of the parts causes the system to effectively cease functioning.

His famous example is the mousetrap. As Behe puts it:

> Typically, such traps have a number of parts: a spring, a wooden platform, a hammer, and other pieces. If one removes a piece from the trap, it can't catch mice. Without the spring, or hammer, or any of the other pieces, one doesn't have a trap that works half as well as it used to, or a quarter as well; one has a broken mousetrap, which doesn't work at all (Behe 2004, 353).

Behe argues that if there are biological systems that are irreducibly complex, they could not be explained by Darwinism, because each part of the system would be useless from an evolutionary viewpoint until they all came together to fulfill their function. Traditional opponents to Darwinism have always mentioned the eye and the wing, in this regard, and Behe supports those examples. But his best examples come from the make-up of living cells. Take the bacterial flagellum, for example. According to Behe (2004,353), "the flagellum can be thought of as an outboard motor that bacteria use to swim." It consists of what may be thought of as a propeller and a drive shaft, a motor and a power source.

According to Behe (2004, 354), the flagellum has "an intricate control system, which tells the flagellum when to rotate, when to stop, and sometimes when to reverse itself and rotate in the opposite direction." The engine rotates at speeds up to 100,000 rpm. The flagellum consists of 30 or more protein parts and these serve many different functions in order for the flagellum to function. Take even one of these parts away, however, and the flagellum cannot function.

The Darwinist has to argue, says Behe, that the flagellum had to evolve from a bacterium that not only lacked the flagellum but also all the genes coded for flagellar proteins, and that it had to do so in small, gradualist steps, without the purpose of the flagellum being present in any of the steps. Furthermore, not only did each of the parts need to evolve but also each one, on its own, had to fulfill some other evolutionary function on the way for it to persist. Finally, each of the parts had to be gathered in the right location and assembled in the proper way. If even one protein is missing, the motor will not work and the whole cluster would be useless. Behe argues that the claim that the flagellum is intelligently designed is a better and more plausible explanation than the Darwinian one which claims that the flagellum motor is the chance result of a blind, step-by-step process.

Kenneth Miller, a Darwinist, responds that the gradualist evolutionary process might very well be what caused the flagellum. It did develop by chance, he claims. And Miller furthermore claims to have found some independent evolutionary functions for some of the sub-sections of the flagellum, adding support to his claim (Miller 2004). Behe responds that even if it were true that subsections of the flagellum had or could have had independent evolutionary functions, the fact remains that the flagellum as a whole is irreducibly complex. That the wooden platform and the spring on the mousetrap have other functions, he argues, does not lower the irreducible complexity of the mousetrap (Behe 2004). In my judgment, Miller's objection is strong and it weakens to an extent Behe's thesis. Nevertheless, Behe's argument, even in this weakened state, is still a striking challenge to Darwinism. This is where the debate stands at present.

Can Intelligent Design possibly be scientific—especially if it admits ahead of time that it can say nothing about the intelligent force that is being said to cause design? I think such a possibility cannot be ruled out in principle. If Intelligent Design could show that a biological system could not have been produced randomly, then it would be entitled to having scientific status. I do not believe, at this time, however, that it has made a strong enough case that design is in fact a scientific reality. It has not shown, so far, that the flagellum, for example, could not be explained in a Darwinian way. Intelligent Design theory, however, has sparked a fresh debate in the intellectual world regarding the origin of species and this is a good thing.

Furthermore, the Intelligent Design movement has reenergized debates about the nature of science. I agree with Phillip Johnson (1993) that, at the very least, Intelligent Design has placed a wedge between those who identify science with philosophical naturalism (i.e., the view that the only legitimate explanations are materialist, mechanistic, anti-teleological ones) and those scientists who are committed to empiricism (i.e., the view that a for a conclusion to be truly scientific, it must be based on evidence and experimentation). Scientific naturalists win the evolution debate by default. It is as if they are saying that since we know that all the diverse life forms we see on earth were produced in a purposeless, mechanistic way, then some version of Darwinism must be true since it is the only theory that provides a mechanistic explanation. The empiricist, on the other hand, will not draw conclusions without evidence and leaves open the question as to whether or not this or that phenomenon can be explained mechanistically. He or she may or may not think that Darwinism provides enough evidence—but in any case the question is one of evidence. Individual Darwinists disagree over these philosophies of science, but the scientific establishment, in legal battles, and in its official statements, has constantly identified science with the philosophy of naturalism, and one can thank Intelligent Design thinkers for exposing this tendency.

Conclusion

In closing, I have argued that the evidence for Neo-Darwinism is weak. It does not have an explanatory mechanism for change and the fossil evidence does not provide external evidence for the theory. I also have argued that the Intelligent Design has yet to become a viable scientific alternative to Darwinism. At this point, then, one should see Darwinian evolution as an unproven scientific hypothesis. Science books, purporting to sum up where science is at any given time, should say that science does not know how to explain how the diversity of life got here, or how life itself got started. When textbooks discuss the theory of evolution, they should mention, along with the theory's strong points, that the theory has several major flaws. And finally, back to Kierkegaard, the individual should not be making qualitative decisions about the meaning of his or her life, or life itself, on the basis of Darwinian theory.

Notes

[1] The claim that peppered moths in industrial England turned from pale to black (to better hide in trees that became darkened by the death of light coloured lichens, due to air pollution) is now widely recognized as highly questionable or false.
[2] In the interview in the video *From a Frog to a Prince* (1997), Gillian Brown asked Dawkins the following question: "Can you give an example of a genetic mutation or an evolutionary process which can be seen to increase the information in the genome?" Dawkins was silent for 19 seconds until he asked that the tape be stopped. When Dawkins asked the tape be turned back on again, he went on to answer a different question than the original.
[3] The archaeopteryx is an ancient bird that some think is an intermediate between reptiles and birds. Scientists, though, are divided about this and Gould does not mention the archaeopteryx as one of his primary examples.
[4] This passage is somewhat controversial. I am prepared to argue that Stanley is referring both to the fossils of the Bighorn Basin of Wyoming and to the fossil record in general. The main thesis in Stanley's book is that Darwinian gradualism is wrong and that the gaps in the fossil record are not evidence that the fossil record is incomplete but rather are evidence for the punctuated equilibrium (or quantum) model.

References

Behe, M. (2004). Irreducible complexity: Obstacle to Darwinian evolution. In: W.A. Dembski, and M. Ruse, (Eds.). *Debating design: From Darwin to DNA*. Cambridge: Cambridge University Press.

Bowring, S., J. Grotzinger, C. Isachsen, H. Knoll, S. Pelechaty, P. Kolosov. (1993). Calibrating rates of early Cambrian evolution. *Science* 261:1293-1298.

Darwin, C. (1859). *The origin of species*. London: John Murray.

Dawkins, R. (1986). *The blind watchmaker: Why the evidence of evolution reveals a universe without design*. NewYork: W.W. Norton.

—. (1997). Interview. In: Keziah and American Portrait Films, *From a frog to a prince: Biological evidence of creation*. Video.

Dembski, W. A. (2004). The logical underpinnings of intelligent design. In: W.A. Dembski, and M. Ruse, (Eds.). *Debating design: From Darwin to DNA*. Cambridge: Cambridge University Press.

From a frog to a prince: Biological evidence of creation. (1997). Video. Keziah and American Portrait Films.

Gould, S. J. (1980). *The panda's thumb*. New York: W.W. Norton.

—. (1981). Evolution as fact and theory. *Discover* 2:34-37.

—. (1987). Darwinism defined: The difference between fact and theory. *Discover* 8:64-70.
Grassé, P. (1977). *Evolution of living organisms*. New York: Academic.
Hitching, F. (1982). *The neck of the giraffe: Where Darwin went wrong.* New Haven: Ticknor and Fields.
Johnson, P. E., (1993). *Darwin on trial.* 2nd edition. Chicago, Il: InterVaristy Press.
Kierkegaard, S. (1941). Editor's Introduction. In: *Concluding unscientific postscript to the philosophical fragments.* Swenson, D. F. and W. Lowrie, W. (Trans.), Princeton NJ: Princeton University Press.
Lester, L.P. and R.G. Bohlin, (1984). *The natural limits to biological change.* Grand Rapids, MI. Zondervan Publishing House.
Mayr, E. (1967). In: P. Moorhead, and M. Kaplan. (Eds.). *Mathematical challenges to the neo-darwinian interpretation of evolution.* Philadelphia PA: The Wistar Institute Press.
—. (1982). Forward. In: M. Ruse (1982). *Darwinism defended: A guide to the evolution controversies.* Reading, MA: Addison-Wesley.
Miller, K. (2004). The flagellum unspun. In: Dembski, W.A. and Ruse, M. (Eds.), (2004). *Debating design: From Darwin to DNA.* Cambridge: Cambridge University Press.
Moorhead, P., and M. Kaplan, (Eds.) (1967). *Mathematical challenges to the neo-darwinian interpretation of evolution.* Philadelphia PA: The Wistar Institute Press.
Patterson, C. (1979). Letter to Luther Sunderland. In: L. Sunderland, (1988). *Darwin's enigma: Fossils and other problems.* 4th edition. Santee, CA: Master Book Publishers.
Scheele, P. (1997). *Degeneratie: het einde van de evolutietheorie en een wetenschappelijk alternatief: hoe de huidige inzichten van de genetica onthullen dat de hoofdsoorten of typen niet door natuurlijke selectie zijn ontstaan.* Amsterdam: Buijten & Schipperheijn.
Spetner, L. (1997). *Not by chance.* Brooklyn. New York: The Judaica Press, Inc.
Stanley, S. M. (1979). *Macroevolution: Pattern and process.* San Francisco: Freeman.
—. (1981). *The new evolutionary timetable: Fossils, genes, and the origin of species.* New York: Basic Books.
Zuckerman, S. (1970). *Beyond the ivory tower.* London: Weidenfeld and Nicolson.

Chapter Four

Science, Religion and the Illusion of Certainty

Donald J. Lococo CSB

Introduction

The tendency to generate analogies is a behavioural characteristic that is specifically human. Animals cannot do this because they lack the essential capacity for abstraction, which the scholastics tell us is a function of the immaterial intellect. As contingent beings, we live under the shadow of omnipotence. Existing somewhere between the divine and the finite, our relationship with God is an analogy of our experience with other living things. No longer denizens of the garden, we see ourselves as creation's crown. But despite the analogy of our superiority to lesser creatures, we are not their gods. According to Gregory of Nyssa, that we are not God is the most essential characteristic of being human. Yet, we draw towards God in human religious forms, because God is the source of our being. Paradoxically, in the divine Other we seek a human image that we believe is mirrored there.[1] This view of religion stems from a worldview of Christian faith.

Alternatively, in the scientific worldview, living in this half-way position between infinite freedom and non-free necessity, there are many qualities about human nature that, when we attempt to characterize them, or abstract about them from the absolute, we collide with paradox. What follows addresses a fundamental quality of human nature which is the reason organized religion developed in parallel with human civilization, why we willfully relate to God in a free response to the offer of salvation: the paradox inherent in our pursuit of certainty.

In this paper, I argue that the desire for certainty is manifested in several modes of human experience. We pursue moral, scientific, psychological, and religious certainties in our lives, but more often than not come up short of the absolute certainty for which we long. Pursuit of certainty of any kind often results in a showdown with those whose view differs from ours. Instead of achieving certainty, in the process we instead increase uncertainty. In the following I show that the way out of this paradox is in seeking concord in dialogue, where truth emerges in the exchange. The illusion of certainty becomes apparent because the only thing we can be absolutely certain of is that dialogue where truth emerges must be forever ongoing.

Mortal Certainty

The greatest certainty in life, from human experience, is death. As a personal certainty, death is experienced only once. It might be argued that death is not an experience at all because we can never reflect upon our past experience of it. Yet there is no facet of life of which we are more certain. We experience death vicariously in the loss of others, indelibly altering our future outlook about our own end. Loss never goes away. Each of us dies on a daily basis in the loss of the day just spent.

The concept that emerges from the grounding experience of loss is certainty. Loss is the only certainty in life. If so, then the yearning for other certainties extends from it and marks human life at every level we experience it. We look for personal certainty within communal structures. Civilization is the grandest external manifestation of the yearning for certainty. The certainty of a stable food supply and safety from wild animals are not the concern of most people in the First World. These ancient longings are now near certainties, but new fears replace them. Uncertainty in the stock market or incidents of international terrorism easily upset the illusion of certainty we have of a stable life and freedom from the wild. As Helen Keller (1957) said, security is mostly a superstition; it does not exist in nature. The effectiveness of fear as a political tool amply illustrates that certainty also does not exist effectively in contemporary culture.

Religion co-evolved with civilization. The self-revelation of God within religious structures was manifest through human intellect and creativity, and through the need to achieve the certainty of a stable social order. Ancient religiosity of pre-civilized human societies gained sophistication with the evolution of social structures. The need for order and maintenance of the common good found its greatest certainty in civilizations that unified the intentions of both the religious and political leaders. In some cases, the supreme leaders were believed to be earth-based deities of a celestial pantheon. Yet even then, the certainty of death was the overwhelming concern of God-kings. This preoccupation found its most extreme expression in the Pharaohs, preserved in a life-like state, and surrounded with all the accoutrements they would need in the hereafter.

The ancient Egyptians extended the certainty of death to a religious hope of life beyond death.

The notion of an afterlife may even have had pre-human origins. Neanderthal gravesites include tools and food items buried with their dead, suggesting their hope for an afterlife. The Neanderthal also made music in the melodic minor scale from flutes carved from the leg bones of cave bears. These observations suggest a cultural sophistication in *Homo neanderthalensis* that chauvinistically we had ascribed only to civilized members of our own species. In any case, knowledge of death and hope of an after-life are principles common to many religions.

Scientific Certainty

Despite spending our lives pursuing certainty, it is an illusion to believe that absolute certainty is obtainable, at least scientifically. The popular notion that scientific facts are certain is a journalistic myth. Science at best provides us with inductive evidence of ongoing provisional conclusions. Doing scientific research is like trying to catch a firefly. You reach out to where you perceive the truth to be only to see it light up further away down the line of induction. *Scientific fact is only certain in the moment of discovery.* The initial elation soon gives rise to the sober act of placing data into the ongoing line of induction, which never ends.

Our ancestors sought certainty when they first built fortified towns to ensure certain safety, food stores, and shelter from the wild. At each level of human social evolution since that beginning, achieved certainty has never been sufficient. Our ancestors always craved more certainty, enslaved as they were by the problem of induction. Throughout history, civilization employed force of arms to ensure the illusion of safety. In fact, science and technology have always been with us in some rudimentary form. In its modern sophistication, the scientific method has helped us to characterize the causes of death and to seek cures to prevent it, neither of which has changed death's certainty.

However, the illusion of scientific certainty is a modern phenomenon. Religious faith has provided its own kind of certainty. Religion is one of three epiphenomenal constants of civilization, the others being arms and technology. These three have through time replaced each other when the others failed to sustain the illusion of certainty. In the modern era, the success of science and the advance of technology have augmented the effectiveness of warfare, ensuring pinpoint accuracy and annihilation of the enemy. The same advances have also reduced human reliance upon religion. For some today, in the immediacy of pain and sorrow, science seems to provide more certainty than prayers to an unseen God who lets little babies die and the innocent starve. Benedict XVI addresses this phenomenon in his encyclical, *Spe Salve:*

> ... our contemporary age has developed the hope of creating a perfect world that, thanks to scientific knowledge and to scientifically based politics, seemed to be achievable. Thus Biblical hope in the Kingdom of God has been displaced by hope in the kingdom of man, the hope of a better world, which would be the real "Kingdom of God." This seemed at last to be the great and realistic hope that man needs. It was capable of galvanizing—for a time—all man's energies. The great objective seemed worthy of full commitment. In the course of time, however, it has become clear that this hope is constantly receding. Above all it has become apparent that this may be a hope for a future generation, but not for me (Benedict XVI, 2007).

In scientific culture, hope itself has been relegated to the strictures of induction.

Despite scientific and technological advances, our world today is more out of balance and less certain than it has ever been. Certainty, the thing we seek the most, is most elusive, and our methods often prove self-defeating. The chief certainty generated by modern warfare is its continuance as a self-contradictory means for peace. Civilization's quest to create heaven on earth continues in building the perfect machine[2] or finding the perfect cure or through assembling the ultimate database. What engine of the collective consciousness drives this pursuit of absolute certainty? Why do we instead by default achieve its opposite? This is a very old question that has long been entangled with the phenomenon of religion in human culture. What inherent quality of human nature drives us to run for the carrot just out of our reach?

Psychological Certainty

In 1991, I read a book by the physician/psychologist Edward De Bono entitled *I Am Right, You Are Wrong,* (1991) which had a life-changing and affirming effect. Edward De Bono is renowned for developing the idea of lateral thinking, which has proved so useful in promoting creativity in education in many countries of the world. Some people do not abide paradoxes easily, and mistakenly try to solve them. De Bono thoroughly illustrates the fallacy of confrontational thinking as a trap for those who cannot bear paradoxes. Confrontational dialogue in the news media is infectious, promoting negative attitudes and negative pedagogy. The *ad hominem* argument has become so acceptable that deeper thinking cannot be brought to matters under media discussion. The fallacy described in *I Am Right, You Are Wrong* continues to be perpetuated to the exclusion of true dialogue beyond the media, particularly among young university students.

Taking seriously De Bono's practical guidelines for thinking, I wondered why the title intrigued me, notwithstanding what it represented and simultaneously satirized. Was it that I cheered its sarcasm about polarized thinking, or did I secretly approve of its literal sentiment? In short—*Did I read the book seeking to confirm that I* was *indeed right and everyone else was wrong?* This concerned me. I realize now that, although I still acknowledge the fallacy of polarized debate, I know that no matter how I try to eliminate this confrontational attitude from my cogitative habits, it remains my approach to argument. Who argues to lose?

We should expect absolute certainty only in rare instances, e.g., doing arithmetic. There are other truths acquired from experience, essentially informed opinions, of which we are less objectively certain. We believe these are correct regardless of someone else's position and no debate will shake us of that certainty unless they can prove that the opinion of others is better informed. A moderate expectation of certainty is essential for any intellectual pursuing a line of thinking. Rigid certainty, however, leads to intellectual hypocrisy. Sometimes the very person who stands on a soapbox preaching against oppression is, when put in a position of authority, the worst of oppressors. Former smokers are often the most obnoxious non-smokers and advocates of non-smokers' rights. The reformed extremist is often extreme in opposition to extremism. The attitude of certainty brings energy to true dialogue as long as it is flexible enough to be let go of once it meets with overwhelming counter-evidence. When taken to an extreme, certainty is self-defeating and makes dialogue impossible.

However, if I truly embrace the irony of *I Am Right, You Are Wrong*, and acknowledge that anyone who holds an anti-dialectic attitude as their *modus operandi* in life is mistaken, then I *am* right and *they* are wrong. In the end, I inescapably possess the very attitude of those whom I decry. *One cannot* agree *with the fallacy evident in the book's title without joining the very group it satirizes.* And if you *disagree* with it, then you see yourself as right and De Bono wrong. It is inescapable. And to remain neutral is to sit on the fence and to absent oneself from any dialogue.

Religious Certainty

I present this so-far psychologically oriented approach to my topic of the illusion of certainty because it is important for me to establish that this perverseness of human nature is the very crux of what religion addresses. Emerging from the limits of human freedom an inescapable and inherent human tendency persists to do the opposite of what we intend. This tendency goes beyond merely the limits of logic. It is perhaps the most human characteristic of any that distinguishes us from irrational beasts. St. Paul (Romans 7:15,18-19) illustrates this human tendency towards contradictory perverseness:

> I do not understand my own actions. For I do not do what I want, but I do the very thing I hate. … I can will what is right, but I cannot do it. For I do not do the good I want, but the evil I do not want is what I do.

According to St. Paul, it is not the law that establishes the paradigm of human behaviour for us to follow but rather, sin in the flesh that makes the law necessary. Law does not make us into moral beings but instead trips us up by reminding us of our hypocrisy. This perverseness of human nature inclines us towards the opposite of what law directs. Paradox emerges from our limited freedom when we resist the instruction of others. We tug away from prescription and are inclined to do the opposite, whether we intend to or not. When you restrain a one-year-old child from entering a restricted area and do so often enough, you reinforce the very behaviour you decry. Retrieve an escaping child and return her to where you want her corralled, and off she will go again in the forbidden direction. We all learned this childish behaviour because, in fact, our parents reinforced it in us, and we all continue to do it in some form as adults. This paradoxical quality of human nature brings us back to Gregory of Nyssa's observation that we are not God. The solution to the inherent human contradictions we all commit must lie outside of human nature. This is why we seek God who transcends all contradiction.

St. Paul was a brilliant observer of human nature. Why religion exists at all as a human cultural phenomenon is summarized by St. Paul in Romans 7. Religion addresses this perverseness of human nature, and through precepts and provocation seeks to curtail it in the faithful. The eternal problem of religion as a mere human institution is that if we rely upon humans to enforce precepts for the most part religion fails. It fails, and will forever fail, because the human will to address the issue is subject to the very perverseness it intends to resolve. In fact, the will to solve the problem is itself the problem. Hence, inspired by grace, we look to God to save us.

A popular illusion of certainty that we are often exposed to is the so-called conflict between science and religion. Although the dialogue at the scholarly level is amicable and conciliatory, the public often perceives that science and religion are mutually exclusive certainties. Periodically it receives superficial treatment by the media and has at the root of it this "I-am-right-you-are-wrong" paradox. True dialogue between science and religion must seek to avoid this popular standoff, but by seeking conciliation we often instead foment division. It is true that science and religion are distinct, but only because science has an exclusive object of study. In common with theology, science has the universe as its object of study, meaning it excludes the spiritual world from its purview because the latter cannot be measured. Subject to the limits of sense perception, science methodologically *cannot* study God.

Scientific methodology limits science to the study of the finite. The object of science is the measurable, quantifiable, useful, material, or energetic thing whose finitude has the asymptotic possibility of total intellection. The universe is vast beyond human comprehension, but for us it is inconceivable that physical reality could have an infinite size and truth content. Non-practitioners of science have been conditioned by the scientific worldview to believe that all mysteries are inevitably solvable. Therefore, science should eventually reach an end to its study. The scientific worldview holds this to be true, almost as an act of faith. As a result, science possesses some attributes of a religion, minus a personal God. It may take five million years or so, but theoretically the end of science is possible, but the question will remain … is there anything more to know? The truths of science, however, are not merely in the objects known but also in the knower who seeks to learn them. Self-knowledge about the paradox of human nature has no end.

The object of Christian faith, on the other hand, is the transcendent God, *but also* the created universe. Religion's object of worship is an immeasurable and unquantifiable supreme being whose infinity is beyond human understanding. The ground of theology is that God as Being could never have even occurred to us if not for God's self-revelation to humanity as love. Where science and religion meet is in the God-created universe of physical and energetic beings in which science finds its fascination and study.

Dialogue and Concord

Within both these broad disciplines of thought and human experience, there is an essential quality required which makes any civilized discipline possible: concord. However, concord is another elusive firefly just out of reach. Every effort to achieve it seems eventually to slip through our fingers. The essence of concord is true dialogue, because in dialogue we can transcend the paradox of cross-intentions and allow truth to flourish, to show itself (*alethea*) in the midst of expressed opinions. The German philosopher Hans Georg Gadamer summarized the refulgence of truth in dialogue in his seminal work, *Truth and Method*. Gadamer (1989, 368) writes:

> The maieutic productivity of the Socratic dialogue, the art of using words as a midwife, is certainly directed toward the people who are the partners in the dialogue, but it is concerned merely with the opinions they express, the immanent logic of the subject matter that is unfolded in the dialogue. What emerges in its truth is the logos, which is neither mine nor yours and hence so far transcends the interlocutors' subjective opinions that even the person leading the conversation knows that he does not know. As the art of conducting a conversation, dialectic is also the art of seeing things in the unity of an aspect (*sunoran eis hen eidos*): i.e., it is the art of forming concepts through working out the common meaning.

Failing to work out common meaning has too often caused war in history, the failure of government, and the fall of civilizations. Historical acts of division were due to the willful failure of dialogue on one or both parts in seeking concord. The "I-am-right–you-are-wrong" worldview makes religion increasingly irrelevant and has turned science into a pseudo-religious alternative.

It is instructive to note that a consistent pattern to the outcome of every war in history revealed itself in the chaotic recovery that marked the aftermath. The lack of control on behalf of opposing ideologies across the "I-am-right-you-are-wrong" divide inevitably results in chaos. Great good has always emerged from chaos, where the grace of the Resurrection has had its activity.

Good that emerges from evil done tells us something valuable about the paradox of true concord. Dialogue requires civilized stability for it to be possible at all, but paradoxically also needs an unsettling chaotic atmosphere so that strong opinions cannot stifle emerging truth. The midwife of truth acts not on one side or the other of personal certainty, but in the helpless uncertainty of the in-between where concord can flourish.

Musical Concord

The following is a lovely example of order emerging from chaos, great good coming from evil done. On November 16, 1414, a watershed event in the history of religion occurred, which had an irreversible affect upon the future of religion. On the shores of Lake Constance gathered all the ruling princes of Europe, including the Holy Roman Emperor and three rival Popes together with their household staffs and governmental ministers. Their intent was to preserve Christian civilization. There they witnessed and participated in a gathering of all the bishops and princes who were well enough to travel. With them came their ecclesiastical courts including their *scholae cantorum*, and their royal courts with their court musicians. The Council of Constance was not only a watershed event for the Papacy, reuniting it under Pope Martin V—ending the decades old scandal of factiousness and division. It profoundly and irreversibly affected political and economic history as well. It also had a little known secondary effect; it irreversibly changed the nature of music, bringing to full adolescence the High Renaissance in all its musical glory.

Concord has always been the very lifeblood of music. Reinhard Strohm, the Heather Professor of Music at Oxford in 1993, published *The Rise of European Music, 1380–1500*. In this important work, he detailed the changes in music that resulted from the gathering in Constance of musicians and composers from all over Europe. Dedicated to the art of musical concord, the court musicians sang, composed, and performed together. If not for the Great Schism and the Council of Constance, they may never have met and listened to each other's music. Without concord there can be no music, no beauty, and no truth.

While their royal and episcopal masters were seeking concord in council, the court and chapel musicians in attendance in Constance engaged in what was until then the largest gathering of musicians in the history of Europe. The sound of music in the streets of Constance was constant. Beauty overwhelmed and scoured clean the discord that marked the century during the Great Schism. As the town's population increased by ten-fold, people jammed into guest quarters in a radius of several miles. It was the 15th century equivalent of the Woodstock festival.

Strohm contends that in the late mediaeval period, music suffered beautifully from a standoff between the novelty that demonstrated a creative move towards an *ars perfecta*, and the conviction that anything modern was degenerate. The standoff between a hunger for change and a resolve that nothing should change has always marked inter-generational discourse. This paradox persists as a characteristic of modern politics.

The tug-of-war of opposite intentions versus seeking the virtue of the mean together drives human history.

Some personality types thrive in this eternal standoff, which in part is why science and religion always seem to be in opposition. Whether true or not, contention is more journalistically interesting than is concord. Contention attracts the ear of those outside the dialogue, especially the news-hungry public. Buried at the root of the science and religion dialogue, at least in Christian circles, is the perception of the divisiveness of the church, which is less significant than the methodological differences between science and religion. Yet those differences paradoxically continue to enable the kind of dialogue that typified the Council of Constance.

After the long schism ended, and for a brief period of history, religious concord was re-established. For a brief moment at least, in the town of Constance, the Catholic Church enacted the very meaning of the Latin word *constans*: it stood together in unity. The new Pope returned to Rome. The princes returned to their thrones and resumed waring against each other, and events returned to a tantalizingly divisive normalcy. The "I-am-right-you-are-wrong" attitude returned, as it always has.

However, music changed forever. The influence of Flemish polyphony on the Italians, and of French song on the Spanish, raised regional musical composition and performance to a new cosmopolitanism that might not have occurred without the religious division that had brought court and chapel musicians together in the first place. However, despite the concord restored in 1414, within 200 years, the church had returned to factiousness, but in a novel form; not moving towards an ecclesiastical *ars perfecta*, but irreversibly new nevertheless.

Division and harmony are essential elements in any musical composition and performance. The resolution of dissonance into harmony is essential for all human creativity. As opposites, the tension created between them is vital to musicality. The paradox between novelty and stability drives the eros of creativity. Necessarily they define each other, both theoretically and practically. Novelty is essential or else life remains historical plagiarism. The "same old, same old" that has marked many periods of music persists until historical watersheds change everything.

Certain Pleasure

Why do we seek a balance between seeking novelty and a preference for stability? Historically, both division and harmony have marked the human pursuit of certainty. It is in our nature to seek either the mystery of an uncertain future or to prefer the certainty of our divisive past. Either pursuit by itself always fails. The balance between the two rouses concord. Paradoxically, in the collective unconscious, rather than achieve certainty, human nature really wishes to retain division: the comfort and discomfort of the eternal standoff. In the shadow of conscious intent, we unconsciously *seek* loss, the very thing we consciously seek to avoid.

This contradiction should not be surprising. There is scientific evidence supporting it. Recently, neurologists have performed scientific research on the neurological effects of moral outrage, signified by people who are certain that they are right and others are wrong. When the researcher placed a morally outraged person into a magnetic resonance imaging machine (MRI) and measured his mental activity while in the very pique of moral outrage, the brain pleasure centers showed heightened neuronal activity. *Outrage is scientifically measurable as an expression of physical pleasure.* Humans secretly love division, the opposite of what we most desire. In fact, we can become physically addicted to it like an opiate. We either actively seek division or unconsciously generate it for pleasure. As the MRI data suggests, we are passionate about it. If not for continual moral outrages to storm about, some of us *cannot* be happy. We now are able to recognize that widespread righteous indignation expressed after important public figures make politically incorrect statements is a form of applause.

Divisive Concord

The Protestant Reformation divided the church seemingly irreversibly into the same national factions that had fuelled the division of the 14th century, but the Holy Spirit worked yet another miracle of unity, one less visible to ecclesiastical form or effective political stability, a novelty nonetheless that has also changed the world forever. The word "Reformation" is one of the most ironic in historical nomenclature. The church was not so much reformed, but rather the human propensity for division took a new form. However, out of this new form of division a novel phenomenon emerged: the birth of modern science. Copernicus presented his heliocentric theory of the cosmos and received a generally positive response from the Catholic Church. He died in the Church's good graces, but still required the promotion of his ideas by a Protestant country for his book to be published. Within less than a century, the political climate of the Catholic Church in the post-Tridentine period was much less tolerant of scientific novelty and reversed its view of Copernicus. The same heliocentric theory that was welcomed one century earlier put

Galileo under house arrest. Similarly, Galileo's later writings, the more influential in terms of their effect upon the progress of scientific methodology, emerged from his period of incarceration in Tuscany, and had to be published outside of papal influence, and again, were widely esteemed in Protestant countries.

In *A History of the Sciences* (1962), Stephen F. Mason proposed that the congruency between Protestant thought and early modern science, and in contrast to Catholic thought, was what led to the development of the scientific worldview and the modern scientific culture. Swiss and German reformers taught that the individual believer should reject the guidance and authority of the priests of the Catholic faith and should seek for spiritual truth in private religious experience. They taught that one should interpret the scriptures for oneself. Similarly, early modern scientists turned away from the systems of ancient philosophers and medieval scholasticism to seek scientific truth in their own experience. They interpreted nature for themselves. The Reformation in religion was reflected in a change in attitude towards a "reformation" of scientific methodology. In both cases, reformers were condemned for abandoning ancient traditions. In each case, they presumed that the conclusions of the ancients, accepted unquestioningly as true for centuries, might be wrong. Pursuing novelty required a schism with the past.

The Calvinists and the early scientists had the same enemy in the scholastic philosophers of the middle ages. The Calvinists attacked medieval theology while scientists attacked their rigid cosmological system, which Copernicus was among the first to suggest was wrong. Both forms of resistance prepared the way for a mechanical/theological worldview. However, this pursuit of novelty led to a new orthodoxy and a new standoff: between biblical literalism and "catholic" hermeneutics of the physical order.

The methodological link between the Protestant movement and the maturation of the scientific method cannot be sundered from basic fundamentals of Protestant thought. In the 19th century, natural philosophy paralleled a kind of natural theology whereby each new discovery was fitted into literal scriptural interpretation that emerged from both the Lutheran and Calvinist reform movements. So when dinosaurs were discovered, the attempt to fit them into the 4000 year history from Adam and Eve to the then-present led to difficulties. Indeed, if species were fixed for all time, the introduction of the concept of evolution into the development of biology as a science was problematic for the Protestant movement, but not for the Catholic world. Catholicism has had more tolerance of evolutionary theories, rejecting only the mutability of the human soul. In part, this tolerance stemmed from the ancient tradition of both literal and figurative interpretation of scripture from the Fathers of the Church, a dangerous kind of creativity. Indeed in the Protestant countries literalism has been a problem that typifies the modern "I-am-right-you-are-wrong" attitude. Protestantism and science were caught up in the beginnings of the same movement—modernity. Neither caused modernity, but are symptoms of it.

Conclusion

Human perverseness is the paradoxical engine that drives creativity and enriches culture. It is messy, dangerous, but largely successful. The generative middle ground within dialogue is essential and must remain in order to "foment" concord. The future of religion requires that we no longer fight paradoxes but rather tap into the creative energy that emerges within the dialogue of opposites, where truth discloses itself despite any dialectical differences.

However, *can* I be certain that I am correct in this conclusion? Am I not motivated also by human perverseness of which I accuse everyone else? Am I right and is the intent of the religion to curtail human perverseness wrong? For religion to be vital as a means of disclosing the truths both divine and human, requires constant dialogue among us, and between us and God. From a Christian perspective, the truth that emerges in dialogue with God is the Divine Logos. According to Gregory of Nyssa, because we are not God, through the *diastema* that separates us from heaven, we seek the Divine Other and find a human image that we believe is mirrored there. Our response to divine reason is a religious one emerging from within a culture that is inescapably scientific. In dialogue, reason emerges in concord. Of that we may not be certain, but we may hope.

Notes

[1] Von Balthasar, Hans Urs, *Presence and thought: An essay on the religious philosophy of Gregory of Nyssa.* Trans. by Mark Sebanc. (San Francisco: Communio/Ignatius Press, 1995). Balthasar sees this separation or "diastema" as the result of creation itself. "There is, in effect, in a created being a fundamental character that at one and the same time reveals to it and hides it from its origins."

[2] The pinnacle of artificial intelligence research will be the creation of the humanoid robot that perfectly resembles and imitates a human being. As a creation in our image, it will possess our frailties as well as its own.

References

Benedict XVI. (2007). *Spe salve*. Retrieved September 2009 http://www.vatican.va/holy_father/benedict_xvi/encyclicals/documents/hf_ben-xvi_enc_20071130_spe-salvi_en.html
De Bono, E. (1991). *I am right, you are wrong: From this to the new renaissance: From rock logic to water logic.* New York: Viking.
Gadamer, H. (1989). *Truth and method,* J. Weinsheimer, and D. G. Marshall (Trans.). New York: Continuum.
Keller, H. (1957). *The open door*. Garden City, NY: Doubleday, 1957.
Mason, S. (1962). *A history of the sciences.* New York: Collier Books. .
Strohm, R. (1993). *The rise of European music, 1380-1500* Cambridge: Cambridge University Press.
Von Balthasar, H. (1995). *Presence and thought: An essay on the religious philosophy of Gregory of Nyssa.* M. Sebanc (Trans.). San Francisco: Communio/Ignatius Press.

PART III

RELIGION AND COMMUNICATION

Introduction

It's easy to overlook the commonplace that communication and community are inextricably linked: the one does much to define the other. Communication, moreover, comprises a wide range of conscious, symbol-laden types and events: interpersonal conversation; mass communication (which now comprises the universe of internet exchange); instruction of any kind; the manifold of imagery, ritual and gesture; artistic performance; even certain kinds of silence. Among the more interesting types of symbol-use are those forms of communication that influence us through the promise of gratification, and persuasion. The two papers in this chapter deal with the religion's place in the widespread social climate of propaganda and the quasi-religious significance of televised food representations.

There are some who say that propaganda is the Siamese twin of religion, but the difficulty with this kind of sweeping statement is that much of what is written about this kind of association is largely anecdotal. In his chapter on the interface between propaganda and religion, Stanley Cunningham undertakes to provide a more *theoretical* framework which will help us to identify religious events and practices that do indeed manifest themselves as recognizable instances of propaganda. Significantly, our modern use of the word "propaganda" derives from an historical organizational event (in 1622) within the Vatican: the establishment of the Congregation for the Propagation *(propaganda)* of the Faith. Modern propaganda, as we now understand it, is really a convenient, shorthand descriptor for a widespread climate of defective communication in which a cluster of inferior cognitive states or episodes (e.g., mere attention, opinions and impressions, unsupported belief, information overload, confusion; error and outright falsity) substitutes for superior epistemic values (e.g., rational argumentation, logic, truth and truthfulness, validity, evidence, understanding and knowledge). Cunningham identifies three areas in the history of religion's allegedly communicative sphere where certain kinds of action reveal themselves as indistinguishable from generally acknowledged propaganda practices: infallible or quasi-infallible utterances; the dampening of intellectual quests and rigorous examination; needless censorship. As Charles Kimball has written, the first of these, the absolutist stance, generally lies behind the other two. Cunningham concludes that a *theory* of propaganda also helps to distinguish genuine instances of religious propaganda from unwarranted attributions of propaganda that only serve to disfigure religion

The association of religion with food is historic and universal: e.g., eating forbidden fruit in the Garden of Eden; manna for God's wandering tribes in the desert; dietary taboos and prescriptions; the sacrament of Communion; food sacrifices and libations; religious feasts and feast days; the deadly sin of gluttony; fasting and abstinence; the metaphor of spiritual nourishment. Drawing upon both loosely structured observations over a period of time and six-weeks of dedicated research, Renée Bondy undertakes to disclose what she sees to be "religious aspects and overtones of food-television" programming. She does so by identifying similarities between characteristic elements of religion (such as ritual and community, sacred places) and several instructional TV cooking programs. The reader may find herself provoked to ask a number of questions: Are these similarities between a particular communication format and conventional aspects of religion anything more than analogous? Does the viewing of pop-cultural, food-programming offer anything at all like a spiritual substitute for religious fulfillment? Do these kinds of media presentations offer us a clue to the religious impulse? The German philosopher Ludwig Feuerbach wrote that "we are what we eat." Does this have even deeper religious implications for TV food presentations?

Chapter Five

Reflections on the Interface between Propaganda and Religion

Stanley B. Cunningham

In December of 2005, I came across the following statement in a letter posted on a web page: *"Propaganda and religion go hand in hand*, it seems; perhaps it's time to denounce both."[1] I'll refer to the first part of this statement, in italics, as the P/R claim. I begin with this statement because it seems to express a widespread sentiment, one that is often thrown out in conversation, but not always so easily captured on the wing. I will use the P/R claim as a convenient springboard for setting out a few of my own reflections on the interface between religion and propaganda, and a possible theoretical direction that these reflections might take.

How does one cope with such a wholesale claim? Ignore it? Dismiss it as the reaction of someone disenchanted by past religious exposure, who now seeks easy verbal payback? But then I was struck by the fact that the writer did not equate religion with propaganda—though I've heard people say that too, just as I've seen and heard people say that all politics (or political discourse) is propaganda, and just as I've read that all communication is propaganda (e.g., Edelstein 1997). Rather, what the writer said is that "propaganda and religion go hand in hand," and there's just enough of a difference in that linkage of two broad notions to rescue it from outright tautology, and to win my attention. Unlike the rest of the P/R statement, however, I don't have much appetite to "denounce both" propaganda and religion. For now, it's the twinning of propaganda and religion that has caught my interest. After all, these are not merely abstract, inconsequential notions: As the current world scene indicates, they spill over all too quickly into social conflict and bloodshed.

Some Remarks on Propaganda and Religion in General

Most of us have some notion of what religion is about. Even if we're not too clear about the general concept of religion, we probably have some direct, experiential connection with religious belief and practices. But there appears to be more uncertainty about what the term "propaganda" means. I've argued elsewhere (Cunningham 2002) that propaganda is a vast and complex modern, social phenomenon, rooted in a series of cognitive disorders in which there is an erosion of superior epistemic values (e.g., truth, truthfulness, rationality and sound reasoning, understanding, evidence along with its procedural safeguards, critical review and evaluation) in favour of cultivating lesser epistemic forms (e.g., attention, impressions, belief, images, information bytes or factoids), as well as downright negative states (confusion, ignorance, misunderstanding, error and falsity). Along with other propaganda scholars (e.g., Combs and Nimmo 1993; Jacques Ellul 1973; J. Michael Sproule 1994; Altheide and Johnson 1980), I view propaganda as a widespread malaise that has expanded beyond particular events to the dimensions of an inescapable climate or environment—aided and abetted by mass media, communication technology and news services—with profound, often imperceptible impact on our lives. Propaganda is no longer reducible to intermittent campaigns or to slick techniques and language, and persuasion effects—although it usually entails most of the above, and commonly manifests itself in those kinds of particulars. Propaganda is not even necessarily something intentional, let alone conspiratorial. Admittedly, propaganda often is intentional, but there's a good deal of literature that demonstrates how the routines of corporate production and dissemination do much to transform information from instructive communication into propaganda that serves the interests of the corporate sector.

While nearly all propaganda and communication theorists think of propaganda as a form of *communication*, I also argue that because of its characteristic disservice to truthfulness and healthy discourse, propaganda, though typically embedded in a welter of communication media and formats, is best conceptualized as pseudo-communication or anti-communication (Cunningham 2002). While propaganda practices may initially serve to form and consolidate certain groups (e.g., cults, fundamentalist and fringe groups, terrorist organizations, political alliances, corporate culture), it actually reduces the features of open sharing and social exchange that define healthy communication. Finally, along with Jacques Ellul (1973; 1967), I think that propaganda is primarily a modern, post-World War I phenomenon. While one can easily discern *intimations* of propaganda in eras past, it is primarily a modern development that took root in the early decades of 20th century mass media. Hence, when authors argue that ancient coinage and monuments celebrating the imperial presence, or medieval legends of the saints, or St. Paul's Epistle to the Romans are "propaganda" or "propaganda campaigns" (Cohen 1981; Jowett and O'Donnell 1992; Munson 1972; Taylor 1995), I believe that these authors are much closer to propounding anachronisms than they are to historical truth. Fractional similarities and resemblances, especially when glimpsed through the lens of remote history, do not add up to our modern version of propaganda. Between our modern era, and the ancient and medieval eras, there are large qualitative differences in the message environments, audience formation and access to information—all of which should discourage us from reading propaganda too far back into history.

The Early Modern Origin of "Propaganda"

For all that, however, there is good reason for tracing our modern use of the word "propaganda" and the notion of a concerted propaganda apparatus back to an overtly ecclesiastical event in the seventeenth century: Pope Gregory XV's establishment of the Congregation for the Propagation of the Faith *(S. Congregatio de propaganda fide)* in June of 1622. (Half a century before this, Rome had already established a propaganda commission of three cardinals in 1568). There is, then, a very real historical connection between the term "propaganda" and religion, including its embeddedness within the Church's structure.

However, the first thing to notice about the Roman event is that this initial high-profile use of the term "propaganda" does not signalize rhetorical acts designed to sway audiences and manipulate public opinion. Rather, it names an organizational event, the founding of a ministry dedicated to ensure doctrinal conformity and orthodoxy in its missionary operations within the Church's worldwide religious community. In other words, the Church's primary and direct intention was not mass persuasion as we normally understand it, but rather regulation, control, doctrinal purity and orthodoxy in its missionary operations. This included northern Protestant countries during those post-Reformation years; and doubtlessly this added greatly to the negative connotations that typically cling to the word "propaganda" (Garstein 1992). While control and uniformity are standard features in modern propaganda practices, this earlier manifestation of a Roman propaganda ministry was directed at internal structures and procedures, and not directly an exercise in broadcasting mass persuasion. Nor should these early developments be confused with the modern phenomenon of "bureaucratic propaganda" which is designed to justify a corporation's performance to relevant audiences such as its shareholders (Altheide and Johnson 1980).

What is it About Religion...?

Moving back to the religion side of the P/R claim, most descriptions of propaganda comprise defining features that seem to mirror those of religion. Consider, for example, the often cited definition of religion supplied by cultural anthropologist Clifford Geertz (1966, 4):

(1) a system of symbols which serves to (2) establish powerful, pervasive, and long-lasting modes and motivations in men by (3) formulating conceptions of a general order of existence and (4) clothing these conceptions with such an aura of actuality that (5) the modes and motivations seem uniquely realistic.[2]

The items enumerated above can just as easily identify many of the self-same features that theorists, for years, have used to define propaganda and its relationship to religion: namely, the use of symbols (1); psychological influence or effects (2); the inculcation of general belief states (3); and conceptions of what is real or what really matters (4 & 5). Historically, each of these features has been used repeatedly in definitions of propaganda, and so this way of thinking about and defining religion— elliptical at best—facilitates an uncritical acceptance of the P/R way of thinking. Indeed, nothing encourages that way of thinking more than the widespread practice of defining both spheres primarily in terms of belief and persuasion.

Countering the P/R Claim

Geertz's definition, however, leaves far more out of religion than it includes: a wider sense of meaning, mystery and destiny; a sense of the holy; love of God; devotion, submission, obedience; ritual; the life of virtue; repentance, forgiveness, redemption, salvation; immortality—not to mention the whole noumenal-transcendent realm of spirituality that lies at the heart of religion. That's not too surprising an omission for a social scientist, perhaps, but it still leaves us with the question about what parts of that vast sector we call religion link up with propaganda: preaching? evangelizing? religious art? literature (including scripture, the entire spectrum of religious commentary, religious poetry)? theology, if there is one? religious ideology (construed as a more or less implicit, unexamined or unchallenged belief-system)? edicts, proclamations, encyclicals, fatwas?—in short, the whole collectivity we call "religious practices." Where, too, might we look for religion-as-propaganda's center of gravity? in the leaders and clerics? in evangelists and fundamentalists? in the followers? or in the artifacts and sacred texts...or in all of these? What corner of religion is not propaganda or propagandistic? Are there any kinds of religious discourse that persuade or instruct without being propaganda?

My remarks above expose the dangers of twinning religion with propaganda—two very different categories of human engagement—without specifying what it is that lends itself to such an analysis. There is, assuredly, some room for comparison and overlap but, initially at least, we can't be sure of much more. The whole area of belief seems to be one such common ground or connecting point between propaganda and religion, there may even be an element of the unavoidable and the inevitable within these possible connections. For example, Sproule (1994), a trusted authority on propaganda, ventures this observation:

> Religion shows signs of becoming propaganda whenever clergy are swept up by social issues such that they merge tenets of religious faith with fashionable political policy or ideology....religion will always be an ambiguous source of modern propaganda (127).

That certainly describes some of the extremist Muslims or "Islamists"; nor do we have to look too far afield in the career of Western religions to find equally compelling evidence for Sproule's claim. Sproule's remark has even more heft if we look at the merging of religious tenets or attitudes (e.g., "the perfidious Jews" that once figured in the Good Friday liturgy; the jihadist theme) with broad cultural mind-sets and belief-systems (the culture of anti-Semitism; the surprisingly wide acceptance of the holiness of the suicide bomber in some sectors of Islamic culture).

Notwithstanding these sorts of connections, the weakness of the P/R claim lies in its scattershot extension, in its absence of qualifications. Indeed, the claim that religion and propaganda go hand in hand, as it stands, is itself an act of propaganda. More precisely, the charge is an instance of anti-religion propaganda because in its very generality it aims at discrediting all or most of the religious enterprise without specifying to what sector(s) of religion or religious history the charge attaches. As a too-broad generalization, it remains uninformative enough to fit in with the pattern of epistemic disservice or defective reasoning that generally characterizes propaganda.

In talking about the interface between religion and propaganda, perspective also makes a difference: P/R talk is *about* religion; it operates outside the pale of religion, and qualifies as anti-religious propaganda; whereas if a propaganda claim stems from one religion about another religion (and its "infidels" or heretics), then it qualifies as an instance of religious, perhaps hate, propaganda.

Another qualification is in order. Many propaganda claims and definitions fail to distinguish between propaganda (which works against good reasoning and knowing well), and normal forms of instruction designed to promote clarity and understanding, agreement and harmony. A distinction, therefore, needs to be made between propaganda and benign persuasion adduced through reason, instruction and example (e.g., the promotion of healthy lifestyle and practices, or sound parenting behavior); between benign socialization and enslaving forms of social cohesion. I've not yet found a compelling theoretical defense of that distinction, but I believe that it will probably entail an *ethical* principle as the distinguishing feature.

A more difficult case has to do with the book-length studies that impugn religion and religious faith in general, a literature with a long history. In recent years, there has been a spate of these titles: Richard Dawkins, *The God Delusion* (2006); Michel Onfray, *In Defense of Atheism: The Case Against Christianity, Judaism and Islam* (2007); Sam Harris, *The End of Faith: Religion, Terror and the Future of Reason* (2004). Most recently, Christopher Hitchens has been getting a lot of press with his *god is not Great: How Religion Poisons Everything* (2007). Depending upon the quality of research and reasoning that goes into any one of these sorts of studies, I am hesitant to dismiss any one title or section thereof as a propaganda tract because the research in them is sometimes respectable, the arguments may be telling. A case in point is Sam Harris's *New York Times* bestseller: *The End of Faith* (2004). Harris bolsters his account with historical and textual research, and a sequence of serious arguments, philosophical and otherwise. While certainly not immune to counterargument, I'm disinclined, by reason of its professionalism and seriousness, to dismiss his work as propaganda. I'm not so sure that the same can be said for Christopher Hitchens's more inflammatory screed, *god is not Great*. Taken collectively, however, the rash of anti-religious, atheistic literature in recent years can be interpreted as a propagandistic assault upon God and religion. I say that because it's easier to discern the outline of a propaganda movement when the literature is polemical, and when it reaches a certain volume; and when, as I shall argue shortly, it is so one-sided and leaves so much out.

Possible Areas of Investigation

These broad rejoinders and distinctions, however, don't let religion(s) completely off the hook. Since much or most of the P/R interface has been handled largely in anecdotal fashion, I would now like to suggest, in outline only, a theoretical direction that future analysis of the religion/propaganda interface might take. I've already indicated in my earlier remarks that the concept of propaganda needs to be understood in terms of epistemic disservice, that is, as something arising from significant deficits in knowing and reasoning. Thus, I propose that we look at this whole question of propaganda/religion interface, linkages (or parallels) in those areas where the management or mishandling of religious truths is likely to converge with recognizable propaganda practices. I have in mind three inter-related categories of religious expression where some of the more recognizable forms of propaganda are visible: (1) religious tenets or truth-claims handled in an absolutist fashion; (2) the practice of promoting unexamined or not-to-be-examined beliefs; and (3) the severe censoring of investigation and communication. I say "inter-related" because all three categories often manifest a certain kind of intellectual misbehavior which, in turn, stems from an absolutist stance. By "absolutist" I mean any pronouncement, utterance or text which presents itself as unimpeachably authoritative, and which forbids or discourages counter-claims, and alternative reasoning and approaches. According to religion scholar Charles Kimball (2003), the whole area of absolutist truth claims and what he views as destructive theological certainty, constitutes one of several warning signs or causes of religion's descent into darkness and harm. He writes:

> While truth claims are the essential ingredients of religion, they are also the points at which divergent interpretations arise. When particular understandings become rigidly fixed and uncritically appropriated as absolute truths, well-meaning people can and often do paint themselves into a corner from which they must assume a defensive or even offensive posture. With potentially destructive consequences, people presume to know God, abuse sacred texts, and propagate their particular versions of absolute truth (46).

Interestingly, too, because of its causal relationship to the other signs that Kimball identifies, this is the first of the danger signals that he singles out for discussion. Let me also add parenthetically that I also believe that at least two of the three inter-related categories of religious expression I have identified above (#2 and #3) could even be viewed as instances or results of bad theology. I hasten to add that in all three cases the misbehavior usually tends to originate with certain individuals or power groups, and is not necessarily a feature or practice supported by the wider religion and all its members.

I have selected these three categories above as convergence points between propaganda and religion because they provide both a theoretical and historical framework for studying how religious authorities and their practices sometimes mirror, imitate, parallel or exemplify the kinds of truth-(mis)treatment that define the heart of propaganda. Adopting this framework now enables us to move beyond the mere enumeration of instances and events to a more grounded and, therefore perspicuous level of understanding of the P/R connection. At the same time, I continue to use the more qualified language of "mirror" and "parallel" and "linkage," because at this point, for purposes of discussion, I'm willing to allow that what is involved may only be parallels or resemblances, and not necessarily outright identity, since that too is worth looking at.

In the discussion that follows, I confess that most of my examples are drawn from Roman Catholicism only because they happen to be ones I'm most familiar with.

Religion, Possessing the Truth, and Infallibility

I take it that most of the major organized religions rest upon truth-claims, revealed by the divine principle, and/or formulated by sages, emissaries or prophets, and that in many cases the revealed truths are held by the faithful to be incontestable. The possible relationship or connection to propaganda lies not so much in the content or truth of this or that proposition (e.g., God shall punish sinners and apostates, and reward martyrs), but rather in the features of incontestability and rigidity with which the proposition is promulgated. Such absoluteness may be vested in sacred texts (e.g., Qur'an; the Bible, the Book of Mormon, Nicene Creed) or in the leader (the Pope in matters of faith and morals, a cult leader [e.g., Jim Jones], the Ayatollah); and the absoluteness then carries over into interpretations, requirements and prohibitions arising therefrom (e.g., Virgin Mary's perpetual virginity and her bodily assumption into heaven; the evil of homosexuality; the sinfulness of birth control; the inappropriateness of certain dietary acts). Furthermore, while infallible pronouncements may be rare (as they really are in the case of Roman Catholicism), the aura of infallibility has a way of spreading imperceptibly throughout the dogma sector. Thus, theologian Hans Küng (1971) writes: "The claim to infallibility in the Church is always present subliminally, even when not given formal expression" (28), and he cites as an example the encyclical *Humanae Vitae* for its apodictic rejection of artificial birth control. In any case, religious absolutes such as infallibility or the inerrancy of sacred texts and their translations, and even the lesser variants of we-know-what's-best-for-you are virtually indistinguishable from the privileged we-know status claimed or implied by many a propaganda source. Typically, propaganda sources—recall the Nazi Ministry of Enlightenment and Propaganda, the elaborate Soviet propaganda apparatus or the implacable authoritarianism in today's North Korea—state or insinuate that *only* they offer the truth, and to this end will adduce authorities, statistics, and oftentimes a bewildering array of information and narratives (even pseudo-science) to underpin such impressions and to secure assent. In extreme cases, religious certainty takes on the character of a self-sealing monopoly: The religion or cult is the sole keeper of the flame, differing beliefs are false, and, by extension, there is no salvation or beatitude for outsiders. When religious leaders exercise this kind of dogmatic control, their affirmations are indistinguishable from propaganda.

Religion and the Discouragement of Investigation and Speculation

In both propaganda and religion, one can find patterns wherein alternative explanations or theories, which challenge absolutist claims, are either ignored or silenced, and the work of critical reasoning and investigation is discouraged in the service of unwavering obedience. Discouragement may take the form of an attitude: e.g. anti-intellectualism ranging from Tertullian's "What has Athens to do with Jerusalem?" (Gilson 1955, 44), to the Christian devotional classic, *The Imitation of Christ*, attributed to Thomas à Kempis. Or it may express itself in the fundamentalist tendency to restrict learning and wisdom to the Bible, or in the militantly conservative and hate-inducing curricula in some madrassas (*The National Post*, May 25, 2006, A27); or in the privileged status of the cultist group leader and his *ipse dixit* pronouncements. Historically, anti-intellectualism in religion has also expressed itself in dogma-based opposition to scientific investigation and rational evidence, most notably, the Galileo debacle, hostility towards scientific evolution, and today's pseudo-science of Creationism. The efforts of some to reconfigure the creation narrative in Genesis as a scientific account in competition with the science of evolution strikes me as being a serious epistemic disservice which, in conjunction with its widespread dissemination by Christian fundamentalists, makes it a clear case of religion-as-propaganda.

The dampening of rational investigation and speculation by the religious hierarchy has a long history, as well, in the areas of theological and philosophical speculation. I had some direct personal experience with this: as a young philosophy instructor at a Catholic university in Ohio in 1960, I discovered that the works by Descartes and Immanuel Kant were stored behind lock and key in the library. In order to assign readings by Descartes and Kant to my students I was told that I would require formal permission from the diocesan chancery office. (Instead, I handed out mimeographed excerpts.) There are other and better-known examples. St. Thomas Aquinas, the patron saint of Catholic schools and universities, died on the way to Rome to answer charges of heresy. For centuries, too, the Roman hierarchy was, if not always hostile to, certainly suspicious of, non-Catholic theology. Again, Catholic clerics, teachers, figures in authority, and recipients of Pontifical degrees were required to profess Pius X's "The Oath Against Modernism" (1910; rescinded in 1967), an embarrassingly conservative prohibition directed against a wide range of "modernist" attempts to interpret and reconsider Catholic dogma. Not surprisingly, in the area of biblical scholarship, there have been patterns of resistance to critical historical studies that threatened to revise older interpretations or validate others.

While one might hesitate to describe these attitudes and patterns as constituting actual propaganda practices, and I dare say that they were never intended to function as such, the authority and strictures exercised in these areas often align themselves with standard propaganda organizations and practices.

Silencing and Censorship

As with distortion and outright falsification, censorship is one of the most commonly cited propaganda practices. Propagandists and their ministries view the exclusion of unwelcome information, language and imagery as an essential part of their job description. Only here the resistance is more radical than discouragement and monitoring: it now involves outright suppression and exclusion of certain kinds of information and images. Extensive state censorship mechanisms were an integral part of the Nazi and Soviet communism eras. They still exist today, worldwide, in state ministries and departments (e.g., Iran, North Korea) just as they always have during wartime in western democracies, usually with a seemingly innocent title such as Ministry of Information or Office of War Information or Joint Information Bureau.

There are enough cases of such exclusion by religions and churches and theocracies to warrant comparison and citations. I'll settle for briefly mentioning a few that I am more familiar with. Two that still existed well into my early adulthood were the Vatican's *Index of Forbidden Books* that lasted more than three and a half centuries (1606-1966) although the principle of a list of prohibited readings was formulated as early as 1515 at the Fifth Lateran Council; and the American Catholic Bishops' Catholic Legion of Decency (1936-71).

The list of excluded authors in the *Index* constitutes a standard course-reading list in the history of modern philosophy: Bruno, Descartes, Pascal, Kant, Hobbes, Berkeley, Malebranche, Schopenhauer, Nietzsche, Bergson, Sartre, et al.; and in modern and European literature: Erasmus, Daniel Defoe, Milton, Dumas, Zola, Graham Greene, Kazantzakis. Curiously, the *Index* did not list Hitler's vitriolic *Mein Kampf*. Sometimes, too, the Church's censoring has been more personal and draconian: consider for instance Rome's silencing of, and forced recantation by, the Jesuit paleontologist Teilhard de Chardin, S.J. in 1925; and, more recently, the exclusion of theologian Hans Küng from teaching in Catholic seminaries.

Most histories of American film will make the point that the Legion of Decency exercised powerful control over the content and fortunes of film production (Walsh 1996). In some churches, Catholics were urged to stand up and pledge obedience to the Legion's ratings. Until the 1960s, when Catholic viewers began to ignore its ratings and proscriptions, a "C" (for "Condemned") rating was often enough to block a film's distribution, and kill off revenues.

In both types of censorship, the Church's motive was ostensibly benign: to prohibit the publication and dissemination of offensive material, and to protect viewers/readers from intellectual and moral corruption.

Censorship has been and still is a commonplace device in other religions. Philosopher Baruch Spinoza was excommunicated from the Amsterdam synagogue for perceived atheism/pantheism. Among a number of Muslim nations there is currently a pattern of severe literary, cinema and music censorship. For example, I read that in Iran there are councils of the Ministry of Islamic Guidance and Culture that monitor every bar of music and all lyrics prior to performance and broadcast. The same is true of poetry and film. Commenting on the widespread suppression of music, Geoffrey Clarfield (2006) remarks sadly that "the affected Muslim nations are literally losing their culture."

Conclusion

It does, indeed, appear that there is a limited justification of the P/R claim. However, rather than rely only upon mere generalization and assertions, or upon unframed intuitions of such instances, I have argued that it is more instructive if we look for possible P/R connections *within a theory of propaganda*: that is, in the direction of religion's treatment of ideas, as well as the related categories of possible information-mismanagement. In this way, the instances of P/R interface that we manage to isolate will appear more readily identifiable and therefore as more compelling instances of P/R because they will have been shown as aligning themselves with the feature of epistemic disserve or deficit that defines the heart of propaganda. Using the categories of truth-mismanagement—infallibility, anti-intellectualism, censorship—I have argued that we can distinguish more confidently between mere parallels or resemblances and real instances of propaganda.

At the same time, it is no less important to recognize that there is a second benefit to this approach: Working within a theoretical framework also serves to limit the sphere of P/R interface to what is *demonstrably* propaganda, thereby protecting whole sectors of religious practice from unwarranted claims of propaganda that serve only to disfigure the religious enterprise. Preaching a sermon, publishing a religious text, and religious instruction do not of themselves constitute propaganda. Only when there has been a demonstrable mismanagement of information and ideas of the kind indicated above can we affirm the propaganda connection.

As a corollary, I also think that the absolutist stances adopted by some religionists (anti-intellectualism and censorship) reflect bad theology. It is bad theology when assertion, dictate, and prohibition prevail at the price of sober reflection and discovery. The medieval theologians adopted as their motto a phrase from St. Anselm: "faith seeking understanding" (*fides quaerens intellectum*), and those words served as a standing invitation to Christian thinkers to expand their theological, philosophical and scientific horizons. St. Albert the Great (1200-1280), the teacher of St. Thomas Aquinas, was an outstanding example of this kind of knowledge enrichment in the thirteenth century. It has always seemed to me that any theology or religion that seeks to suppress the mission of deepening our learning in general, and the understanding of one's faith in particular, also undertakes to frustrate God's own design and handiwork: namely, the human person's innate appetite for understanding and knowledge. Propaganda can thwart this appetite in religion, and by using religion, as much as it does, in other sectors of our culture. In a world where religion can all too easily be exploited and misappropriated in the service of cultural and political rivalries, we need to become more adept at differentiating between religious thought and practice, and the disfigurements wrought by propaganda.

Notes

[1] Mat Rhodes (Medford) in *Mail Tribune*, Dec. 12/05 (Southern Oregon's News Source, mailtribune.com.), accessed on Dec. 23, 2005.
[2] I am grateful to Professor Brian Patrick of the University of Toledo for bringing this definition to my attention.

References

Altheide, D.L. & J .M. Johnson (1980). *Bureaucratic propaganda*. Boston, MA: Allyn and Bacon.
Clarfield, G. (2006). Of Muslims and music. *The National Post*, Dec. 6, A23.
Combs, J.E., and D. Nimmo. (1993). *The new propaganda: The dictatorship of palaver in contemporary politics*. New York: Longman.
Cunningham, S.B. (2002). *The idea of propaganda: A reconstruction*. Westport, CT: Praeger.
Cohen, E. (1981). The propaganda of the saints in the middle ages. *Journal of Communication* 31: 4, 16-26.
Edelstein, A. (1997). *Total propaganda: From mass culture to popular culture*. Mahwah, N.J.: Lawrence Erlbaum.
Ellul, J. (1973). *Propaganda: The formation of men's attitudes*. New York: Random House.
—. (1967). *Histoire de la propagande*. Paris: Presses Universitaires de France.
Garstein, O. (1992). *Rome and the counter-reformation in Scandinavia*. Leiden: Brill.
Geertz, C (1966). Religion as a cultural system. In: M. Banton (Ed.), *Anthropological approaches to the study of religion,* 1-46, London: Tavistock.
Gilson, E. (1955). *History of Christian philosophy in the middle ages*. New York: Random House.
Jowett, J & V. O'Donnell (1992). *Propaganda and persuasion.* 2nd edition. Beverly Hills, CA: Sage.

Kimball C. (2003). *When religion becomes evil.* San Francisco: Harper.
Küng, H. (1971). *Infallibility? An inquiry.* New York: Doubleday.
Munson, G. (1972). *Twelve decisive battles of the mind.* Freeport, N.Y.: Books for Libraries Press.
National Post. (2006). "What Saudi students learn." May 25, A27.
Sproule, M.J. (1994). *Channels of propaganda.* Bloomington, IN: EDINFO Press and ERIC
Taylor, F.M. (1995). *Munions of the mind: A history of propaganda from the ancient world to the present era.* Manchester, UK: Manchester University Press.
Walsh, F. (1996). *Sin and censorship: The Catholic church and the motion picture industry.* New Haven, CT: Yale University Press.

CHAPTER SIX

FEEDING THE SOUL: FOOD, TELEVISION AND FAITH

RENÉE BONDY

Introduction

From cannibalism to consecration, from asceticism to hedonism, from mendicants' begging bowls to Christmas dinner, food bears countless, inextricable ties to religion and its institutions and rituals. Some of these connections are obvious and conventional, while others are more subtle and unorthodox. By examining the recent phenomenon of food-television,[1] I will argue that the notion that our television viewing fills a spiritual desire is not so farfetched in the 21st century. As spiritual seekers become increasingly comfortable seeking fulfilment beyond the doors of established institutions, we may just be more and more willing to swallow new and exotic fare in order to satisfy our spiritual hungers.

First, this essay takes a brief look at the distinct relationships between religion and television, and religion and food, and this will set the stage for a more in-depth overview of the ways in which scholars of the late 20th and early 21st centuries have assessed the place and purpose of food-television. The second part of this paper will analyse food-television in light of its manifest religious characteristics and qualities. What I propose is that food-television programming addresses numerous aspects of religious experience and that, albeit unconsciously, viewers are drawn to food-television in order to fulfil spiritual needs that are perhaps not met through other explicitly religious venues. I will conclude with some suggestions as to what we can learn about the future of religion by close examination of such late 20th and early 21st century trends in popular culture.

Religion, Television and Food: Some Contemporary and Historical Recipes

When we think about the intersection of religion and television, perhaps the first thing that comes to mind is Billy Graham-style evangelical preachers; or PBS and CBC documentaries; or new speciality channels, such as Canada's interfaith "Vision TV" or the Catholic "Salt and Light Television." Or maybe we think about popular television shows such as the comedy *The Flying Nun* (1967-70) or, more recent programs such as *Touched by An Angel,* or BBC's *The Vicar of Dibley.* The Food Network or, in Canada, Food TV, is not a place that most people turn to for religious inspiration, at least not consciously.

Television has a curious relationship with the subject of religion. As Canadian writer Michael Higgins has noted, religion has been marginalized in the mainstream media, that is, treated as "an unreflected, unmediated, often trivialized subject." There is an irony, Higgins claims, that while the producers of media are discovering that "religion sells, that spirituality is meaningful, they are ill-equipped to deal with the renascence of public interest" (Higgins 2000, 31). If indeed, as Higgins would have us believe, the mainstream media are unreflective in their treatment of religion, and if there is an abiding interest among the viewing public, it would seem conceivable that religion and its many thematic descendents might arise in seemingly innocuous programming and in unexpected forms, such as food-television.

At the same time, a study of food-television must acknowledge that there are countless intersections between the subjects of religion and food, and many scholars have explored these and have drawn persuasive and engaging conclusions about this ancient and enduring relationship. A few salient examples from historical writing demonstrate the depth and range of such inquiry. Reay Tannahill's classic work *Food in History* (1988) offers insights into the many religious taboos and ritual prescriptions found across the world's religions, including explanations of ancient, Hebrew dietary laws and the principles of Jain and Buddhist vegetarianism. The ascetic and ritual practices of religious women in medieval and early modern Europe are probed in Rudolph Bell's (1985) *Holy Anorexia* and Carolyn Walker Bynum's (1987) *Holy Feast and Holy Fast*; and these histories raise key questions regarding the place of food in a female Christian spirituality. Both Bell and Bynum argue that radical asceticism was a means by which women might gain control of their bodies and their souls, thereby more fully partaking in the ritual food and spiritual sustenance of an otherwise male-oriented Church. Such scholarship, however, raises many intriguing questions regarding the control of women's bodies, the use of food as power and currency, and internalized misogyny in the lives of sainted and saintly women. More recently, Daniel Sack, in *Whitebread Protestants,* argues for the centrality of food to the faith of American Protestants, noting that "their eating practices reflect their understandings of ritual, community, hospitality, and justice," and that food has "important and multiple meanings" relative to these understandings (Sack 2000, 7).

The aforementioned works of Tannahill, Bell, Bynum and Sack are a mere slice of an extensive and global history of food and religion which encompasses nearly all religious traditions and experiences. Note that even a very brief sampling of the historical research indicates food's influence on our understandings of ritual, regulation, gender, community and other social phenomena. So, where might an examination of the religious aspects of food-television fit into this history, and why is it important?

Let us examine the phenomenon of food-television, its popularity and the various ways in which we might assess the genre. My own interest in this topic was sparked by an intriguingly titled article in *Harper's* by Frederick Kaufman: "Debbie Does Salad: The Food Network at the Frontiers of Pornography" (Kaufman 2005). Kaufman draws numerous comparisons between the genres of soft porn and food-television, including striking similarities in cinematography and sound, the air-brushed perfection of tempting products, and the raw sensuality of the subject matter. Initially, I found Kaufman's argument quite persuasive: Food does seem to be a commodity that is easily sexualized. I had to admit that maybe my own addiction to cooking shows has somewhat romantic, if not erotic, overtones!

This notion of food as the "new pornography" was raised in Britain in the late 1990s with a sensational study at Bournemouth University which sought to record and analyse people's erotic responses to food imagery. These researchers noted that while we cook far less than in past generations, we tend to "ogle" and "lust after" images of food in glossy magazines and on television. Bordering on a kind of fetishism, "gastro-porn," while enticing and engaging, has its limitations as "consumer porn that is a substitute for real sensation" (Hughes 1999). *Toronto Star* columnist Bill Buford's take on food porn is that "it's not erotic. . . . that's not why it's called food porn. It's just unreal. You will never meet a Playmate of the Month; you will never eat the red, juicy tomato that you see on *Barefoot Contessa*" (Buford 2006). Buford hints at an artistic eroticism implicit in food programming, a more sophisticated and somewhat less raw interpretation of the sexuality of food.

Still, in contemporary food-television programming, "gastro-porn" images and rhetoric are common. Note the recent popularity of Giada De Laurentiis's *Everyday Italian*. One reviewer describes De Laurentiis as "lithe and young and pretty, a prettiness that no Food Network executive is going to allow her to hide behind an apron…She…[has] a diaphanous dress sense, occasionally looking as though she'd just come from bed or was about to return to it" (Buford 2006). Canada's Food TV Network uses explicit reference to the erotic in its marketing of *Nigella Feasts*, starring the rubenesque Nigella Lawson, claiming "Food has never been this sensual!"

Yet the more I thought about Kaufman, Buford and others' appraisals of "gastro-porn," the more I began to think that there is probably more to be said about our fascination with food-television. Certainly, our desire to watch beautiful celebrity chefs as they shop, prepare, cook and dine borders on a kind of voyeurism, and the food-television industry has certainly capitalized on the well established tenet, "sex sells." But what is the true, underlying force behind our fascination? Is it sex, or is it something even more essential?

Several other researchers have examined the food-television phenomenon through various lenses. Some consider food-television, along with other lifestyle-programming, such as might be found on Home & Garden Television or the Life Network, to be merely one expression of 21st century consumerist mentality. Mark Meister, Professor of Communications at North Dakota State University, argues that American capitalism is driven by commodification and consumption, and that the TV Food Network's promotion of the "good life" and its accompanying rhetoric serves to encourage "the feeding of excesses in modern culture and promotes waste, indulgence and gratification" (Meister 2001, 166). Others take a somewhat softer and less judgmental view, noting that food preparation, once necessary for survival, has now been converted into a leisure activity. As Canadian food columnist Lucy Waverman observes, cooking, "like gardening, [is] a hobby, an activity, even an art form" (Waverman 2001). And, as many have argued of post 9/11 America, Karen Gelbart, vice-President of programming for Canada's Food Network notes, "in the aftermath of September 11th, people are spending more time at home with family and friends," inspiring new interests in food and cooking (Smith 2002, 16).

Food Network Television and Faith

My inquiry into the religious aspects and overtones of food-television is based on my own viewing, some casual and some intentional and purposeful. In other words, my tendency over the past two years has been to watch Food TV for about one hour per day. In preparation for the writing of this paper, I engaged in more systematic viewing, watching three thirty-minute programs per day, five days per week for approximately six weeks. The three programs to which I will refer in the remainder of this paper—*Everyday Italian, Chef at Home,* and *Barefoot Contessa*—are representative of "traditional domestic instructional cooking programs" on Food TV today (Ketchum 2003, 223), and their hosts, Giada De Laurentiis, Michael Smith and Ina Garten, are among the more well-known chefs on the network. Also, in keeping with the conventions of the domestic instructional cooking programs as described by Cheri Ketchum,[2] these shows are hosted mainly by women. Their sets feature visually appealing and softly lit traditional kitchens; they showcase active, hands-on cooking enhanced by means of intimate camera-angle shots of food; and they feature a chef who engages directly with the audience and who talks specifically about cooking for family and friends (Ketchum 2003, 223).

My observations indicate that these programs reveal numerous intersections between food-television and Winston King's descriptions of the characteristic elements of religion. King (2005) argues that "religions adapt their tangible historical forms as matrices of cultural and social elements about the depth-centres of culture." As such, "the beliefs, patterns of observance, organizational structures, and types of religious experience are as varied as the matrices that give them birth, and... they in turn help form and reform." Still, there arise among the varieties of religious life certain characteristics that are "distinctively religious," including traditionalism, myth and symbol, concepts of salvation, sacred places and objects, sacred actions or rituals, sacred writings and sacred community (King 2005, 7696-7700). I will explore four of King's criteria: traditionalism, sacred places, ritual and community—and the ways in which these are manifest in contemporary food-television programming.

The American Food Network, established in 1993 (Meister 2001, 165), is a relative newcomer to the highly competitive world of late 20th and early 21st century broadcast media. Even if we were to include pioneers of the genre, like Julia Child, in this discussion, food-television remains a relatively new phenomenon. While there is limited history upon which to establish an argument for traditionalism in the genre, domestic instructional cooking programmes intentionally employ language and activities which harken to earlier times and to traditional, home-based food preparation. *Everyday Italian, Chef at Home,* and *Barefoot Contessa* feature traditional kitchen settings; Michael Smith, of *Chef at Home,* cooks from his kitchen in his home on Prince Edward Island. The post 9/11 trend toward home cooking and entertaining is modelled and encouraged with such settings, and a back-to-basics, do-it-yourself ethic underscores this trend. *Chef at Home's* opening theme music incorporates the repeated phrase, "You can do it too!," drawing the viewer into the world of home cooking.

Not only does the setting of domestic instructional cooking shows encourage traditionalism, it also elevates the home as a sacred space. *Barefoot Contessa's* Ina Garten regularly sings the praises of her country home in the Hamptons, and Michael Smith of *Chef at Home* extols the beauty and simplicity of life in rural Prince Edward Island. Fine dining and special-occasion entertaining, once relegated to up-scale restaurants and exclusive catering services, are afforded a place in the homes of these chefs and, presumably, those of their viewers. The exclusivity and prohibitive costs of the dining experience are reduced in lieu of the intimacy and comforts of home. Further, these events are ritualized. Regular viewers of *Barefoot Contessa* will know that Ina's husband, Jeffrey Garten, a professor at Yale University, returns from the city each Friday evening not to a traditional Seder, but to a lovingly prepared roast chicken dinner (his favourite). The closing scenes of most episodes of *Chef at Home* feature Michael Smith and his family—wife Rachel and son Gabe—gathered at table for the evening meal, discussing the food and its preparation.

Not only is food ritualized within families, but the hosts of contemporary food-television programmes take the viewer beyond the home and into the local community, introducing the viewer to local butchers, bakers, greengrocers, and vintners. The extended family and friends of the chef-host create a sacred community of sorts, a larger social matrix within which the viewer might contextualize the ritualized culinary experience. The viewer meets local Prince Edward Island farmers on *Chef at Home,* and Ina Garten not only takes her viewers shopping for foodstuffs and wine, but also to the local florist. Further, the proprietors of these shops are Ina's frequent dinner guests, which affords a sense of an interactive and interdependent local community. On *Everyday Italian,* Giada De Laurentiis takes her viewers on shopping trips to the local grocer or cheesemonger. She routinely refers to her mother's or grandmother's recipes, and to her childhood memories of meals and celebrations in her

Italian-American family, giving a sense of the intergenerational value of the rituals of home cooking.

Subscribers to Food TV are also encouraged to engage with a larger food community through online blogs on the official foodtv.ca website. Furthering the interactive nature of food-television, such web-based forums extend a sense of community wherein viewers can actively participate in the media culture, providing input and feedback which could, presumably, influence future programming.

Two Key Questions

Two key questions will help to further situate and make sense of these observations regarding the religious characteristics of food-television. First, what general conclusions can be drawn from observation of these recent trends in food-television, and how do these fit into the day-to-day lives of the faithful? Second, what does this genre and its viewership tell us about "the future of religion"?

Most obviously, the recent trends in food-television, particularly in domestic instructional cooking shows, like *Everyday Italian, Chef at Home* and *Barefoot Contessa,* point to heightened interests in food, home, community and ritual, and their sacralization. Although it is difficult to determine whether these interests are attributable to greater focus by government agencies on health promotion and nutrition or to a post 9/11 consciousness, or to the desire for spiritual and social fulfilment beyond the doors of churches and temples, sociological trends indicate the latter. Reginald Bibby's studies of Canadians' religious observance indicate that while a 1945 Gallup poll found weekly attendance at religious services to be at about 60%, by 1975 that number was reduced by almost half; and by 2000, only about 20% of Canadians attended religious services on a weekly basis. This decline was particularly pronounced, notes Bibby, among Roman Catholics and "mainline Protestants—the United, Anglican, Presbyterian, and Lutheran churches" (Bibby 2006). Although attendance has increased in recent years, particularly among youth, to a total of about 25% in 2005, this leaves a Canadian population—84% of whom still claim to identify with a religious group—without a permanent "home" (Bibby 2006). At the same time, according to Canada's Media Awareness Network, Canadians watch about 22.7 hours of television per week (Media Awareness Network, 2007). It would be rather audacious, and without substantiation, to claim that food-television is a "new" religion. In fact, while it enshrines some characteristics of religion (e.g., traditionalism, sacred places, ritual and community), it is difficult to make claims for other key features of religious experience, particularly those which King identifies as "concepts of salvation" (King 2005, 7697). Beyond the promise of physical and emotional satiation, and a general orientation toward fulfilment, broadcast media in any form cannot lay claim to, or be imbued with, genuine salvific ability. Still, observations of food-television and its salient religious characteristics can, perhaps, tell us something about what religious seekers of the present and near future are looking for.

First, observations of a pop-culture trend like food-television indicate that people are seeking fulfilment within their own homes. While fewer Canadians attend religious services, their television viewing also indicates that they are interested in connections between home and local community, and in traditional, family-oriented ritualized gatherings. Second, the rituals they seek are simple—without the grandeur and pretence of formal, conventional religious ceremonies. And, third, despite the desire for simplicity which is evident in such pseudo-religious inquiry, there is also a heightened interest in the sensual, especially in the desire to taste, smell and touch the simple yet sacred symbols of ritual. Finally, I think there is a fourth consideration as I try to make sense of the popularity of food-television, and it is one that is perhaps more implied than proved. It would seem that accessibility is a consideration when we attempt to understand people's relationships to religion. Assuming that viewers are not mere couch-potatoes, and that their viewing is intentional and meaning-filled, perhaps food-television is simply more accessible and digestible than mainstream religious fare.

By way of illustration, consider the story "The Salad Bowl," as told by spiritual writer Margaret Silf in *Inner Compass: An Invitation to Ignatian Spirituality.* Silf recounts her attendance at a celebration at the church hall of a friend. A great pot-luck feast had been assembled and, in a short time, consumed, except for a beautiful rice salad, which remained untouched among the other now-empty bowls and platters. Silf, noticing the uneaten salad, wondered why no one had eaten it, especially since it looked so very appetizing. And then it dawned on Silf—it was obvious why no one had eaten the salad:

> There was no spoon. The fact hit me like a sledgehammer that night. I realized that the salad bowl was telling me something about the Church. It, too, is sometimes like a bowl of salad, full of what people are so longing to receive, so hungry for. But where is the spoon? Shall the treasure remain forever on display, the inaccessible centrepiece of an empty table? Do God's people really have the means to eat the food he prepares for them, or is it wrapped in the cellophane of doctrine and set high on the top shelf of

theology? And are they too well trained to dare to mention the problem? (Silf 1999, ix).

Conclusion

While food-television provides virtual food, vicarious religious experience and pseudo-community—hardly the stuff of traditional religion—an examination of its content and its place in contemporary culture points to unfulfilled desires and a need for accessibility, for "spoons," as it were, in the lives of 21st century seekers. Whether our daily bread is found on the altars of cathedrals or television studios, clearly it remains a staple of our diets.

Notes

[1] I use the term "food-television" throughout this paper to denote the genre of programming provided by the U.S.-based Food Network and the affiliated Canadian specialty channel, Food TV.

[2] Cheri Ketchum (2005, 223), in her analyses of the Food Network's programming, relies on four categories of food programming, which she labels: *"traditional domestic instructional cooking; personality-driven domestic cooking shows; food travel programs;* and the *avant-garde."* It is the first category of programs, *traditional domestic instructional cooking* programs, which I examine in this essay.

References

Bell, R. M. (1985). *Holy anorexia.* Chicago: University of Chicago Press.
Bibby, R. (2006). Who says God is dead? *The Globe and Mail.* April 17, A15.
Bynam, C. W. (1987). *Holy feast and holy fast: The religious significance of food to medieval women.* Berkeley: University of California Press.
Buford, B. (2006). TV dinners: The rise of food-television. *The New Yorker.* November 2. Retrieved February 28, 2007,
    http://www.newyorker.com/fact/content/articles/061002fa_fact
Graham, D. (1999). The joy of looking: Food as gastroporn. *The Toronto Star.* November 17, 1
Higgins, M. W. (2000). *The muted voice: Religion and the media.* Ottawa: Novalis.

Hughes, J. (1999). Food is the new pornography. *The Independent*, October 17. Retrieved from http://www.independent.co.uk/life-style/food-and-rink/news/food-is-the-new-pornography-743699.html

Kaufman, F. (2005). Debbie does salad: The Food Network at the frontiers of pornography. *Harper's.* October, 55-60.

Ketchum, C. (2005). The essence of cooking shows: How the Food Network constructs consumer fantasies. *Journal of Communication Inquiry* 29:3, 217-234.

King, W. L. (2005). Religion. *Encyclopedia of Religion*, 2nd edition. L. Jones, (Ed.) New York: Macmillan, 7692-7701.

Meister, M. (2001). Cultural feeding, good life science, and the TV Food Network. *Mass Communication and Society* 4: 2, 165-182.

Sack, D. (2000). *Whitebread Protestants: Food and religion in American culture.* New York: St. Martin's Press.

Silf, M. (1999). *Inner compass: An invitation to Ignatian spirituality.* Chicago: Loyola Press.

Smith, L. (2002). Who's cooking? *Gifts and tablewares,* Spring 27:2, 16.

Tannahill, R. (1988). *Food in history.* New York: Crown Publishers.

Waverman, L. (2001). A taste of things to come. *The Globe and Mail*, December 29.

PART IV

RELIGION AND MODERNITY

Introduction

In 1610, with the publication of *Sidereus Nuncius,* Galileo initiated the controversy that, for many, continues to stand as emblematic of the relationship between religion and the modern world, or as the relationship is sometimes framed, between faith and reason. While it may be impossible to delineate precisely when a particular era begins, the 17th century, especially as seen in the work and impact of Galileo (1564-1642), Descartes (1596-1650) and Newton (1642-1727), marked a turning point in both science and philosophy that contributed much to shaping the modern era

Some of the salient features that characterize modernity include: a style of reasoning that privileges the scientific and empirical; a focus on individual rights and freedoms, and the democratic procedures that ensure them; prodigious industrial and technological advancements; an increasingly international market economy; and continuing uncertainty about the value and role of religion.

The attitude of religion toward the scientific, political and economic developments of the modern era was often cautious and occasionally oppositional. This led to an incremental marginalization of the influence of religion in the public square, while at the same time religion continued to remain significant in the lives of ordinary citizens. More recently, in many developed western countries, the attitude toward religion has moved to a level of active antipathy, even as, or perhaps because, religion has emerged as an important dynamic in the current geopolitical reality.

The papers that follow address some aspects of religion's encounter with modernity, both from the perspective of modernity's dismissal of religion's validity (Johnson) and from the perspective of a religion's (i.e. Islam) approach to the insights and developments of the modern era.

In his paper Johnson examines the arguments of some of the proponents of the new militant atheism. Johnson first provides a brief history of the relationship between philosophy and religion, and then moves to his critique of some of the atheistic positions put forth in some recent publications. Writing from the perspective of a logician, Johnson examines the content as well as the language and form of the argument. While providing reasons why he finds their positions unconvincing, he also points to indications that the exponents of these positions may not be the dispassionate inquirers they claim to be.

The distinct features that constitute the interaction of Islam and the modern world are the focus of Sadegh Zahedi's presentation. As Zahedi points out, the characteristics of the modern world are a product of Western culture and come to the East as part of a process of colonization. Thus, as Islam engaged modernity it needed to make some distinction between: modern developments, Western culture and colonial perspectives. Moreover, Zahedi reminds us that Islam is not monochromatic and that *within* Islam there are a variety of understandings, interpretations and practices regarding what it means to be a faithful Muslim.

The issues these papers address remain important topics that need serious and thoughtful reflection. All the indications are that religion will indeed have a future and that it will continue to shape values and directions in the choices that the human community will make.

CHAPTER SEVEN

THE UNEASY ALLIANCE: THE ONGOING RELATIONSHIP BETWEEN PHILOSOPHY AND RELIGION

RALPH H. JOHNSON

Introduction

Several recent publications—many of them written by philosophers—have raised anew the question of religion. Prominent among them are: Harris, *The End of Faith*, 2004; Dawkins, *The God Delusion*, 2006; Dennett, *Breaking the Spell*, 2006; Onfray, *In Defense of Atheism: The Case Against Christianity, Judaism, and Islam*, 2007; Stenger, *God: The Failed Hypothesis*, 2007; and Hitchens, *god is not Great*, 2007.

The issue has also been prompted by the recent developments on the world scene, particularly what is called Islamic fundamentalism, and its violent political expression. Here is Dawkins's litany from *The God Delusion*: "Imagine no suicide bombers, no 9/11, no 7/7, no Crusades, no witch hunts, no Gunpowder Plot, no Indian partition, no Israeli/Palestinian wars… no persecution of Jews as Christ killers…" (2006,13). Religion, it seems, is suddenly a hot button issue on the cultural scene.

The question I want to pose here is: Where is philosophy in this discussion? From its very beginning, philosophy has had an ongoing and ambiguous relationship with religion—what I call an uneasy alliance. Where does the situation stand today, just into the 21st century? What, we may wonder, does the future of the relationship between philosophy and religion look like?

I begin with some preliminary remarks about philosophy and religion. Then I provide a rough sketch of the history of this uneasy alliance. Next I attempt to describe the situation today: where do matters stand as far as the relationship between philosophy and religion? What are the new developments? Here I will discuss what is called The New Atheism, and that discussion will form the basis for my attempt to assess future prospects for this alliance.

Preliminary Matters

What is Religion?

It is difficult to answer this question without begging difficult questions. Let me approach this question from the perspective of meaning taken first as extension, then as intension. Within the extension of 'religion' will fall Judaism, Christianity, Islam, Hinduism, Buddhism, etc., and newer phenomena such as Bahai. On the cusp would be a phenomenon like scientology, while clearly outside its extension would be such phenomena as atheism, humanism, Marxism, numerology, etc. Looking now at meaning as intension: In all likelihood, religion is best understood as what Wittgenstein calls a *family resemblance* concept (PI, #67); that is, a concept which is not characterized as designating an essence, a feature that all instances share in common, but rather as referring to a set of features such as a creed, a set of values, rites, rituals, practices, some form of prayer/worship, governance, a public presence, traditions, the possession of some of which will be sufficient to mark something as a religion.

Let me cite here Dennett's definition: "I propose to define religions as "social systems whose participants avow belief in a supernatural agent or agents whose approval is to be sought" (2006,11). Dennett is using his definition to frame his argument that religion should be studied scientifically and that religious people should agree with this and not resist or feel threatened. What bothers me about the definition is the part about seeking approval. Religion seems more a matter of how to live one's life, about what's important, the highest values. The definition cited above is an Old Testament view, or one that applies to Greek folk religion but is not well-suited to Christianity, which is Dennett's focus in *Breaking the Spell.*

Here are some better ways of thinking about religion. According to Rudolf Otto religion has to do with the holy, the numinous. William James, who defends religion in *The Will to Believe* (1896/1956), and *The Varieties of Religious Experience* (1902), characterizes religion in terms of a phenomenology of religious experience. In the latter work, James writes:

> [It is] not religious institutions, traditions and creeds that have, religiously speaking, motivating force for the individual person, but responses to prayers, conversations with the unseen, voices and visions, changes of the heart, deliverances from fear, infusions of help, as well as assurances of support (1902,31).

For a balanced account of religion that takes into account both its weaknesses and its strengths, I recommend Kimball, *When Religion Becomes Evil* (2004).

For the purposes of this paper, I will for the most part restrict my focus to Christianity, for the interpretation of which I will be relying on Kierkegaard, who, in my view, has the clearest position on the nature of religion in general and Christianity in particular. Writing as Johannes Climacus in *Concluding Unscientific Postscript* (1941), he presents Christianity, not as a philosophical system (or worldview), but rather as what he calls an "existence communication" (i.e., an invitation addressed to an existing individual) that expresses an existential contradiction: the fact that God has existed in time. In *Philosophical Fragments* (1941), faith is presented, not as a relationship to a proposition, but rather to a person. Faith is understood, not as a doxastic attitude ("believing what you know ain't so") but rather as a way of life. Faith is the rebirth; the happy passion, the overcoming of offense ("Blessed is he that is not offended in me." Lk. 7:23). This does not sound much like seeking the approval of the distant deity that Dennett mentioned in his definition.

What is Philosophy?

In this paper, I take as my reference point traditional Western philosophy going back to the Pre-Socratic tradition and evolving through the Greek and Medieval periods, then the modern and post-modern eras and on into the present. Philosophy has been described as naked intelligence wrestling with the problems of life. Wittgenstein says that a philosopher is not a citizen of any community of ideas—that is what makes him a philosopher (*Zettel*, #45). Most generally, philosophy might be described as systematic inquiry into the nature of reality (metaphysics), knowledge (epistemology), value (ethics), and methods of reasoning (logic). Historically, there has been an uneasy alliance between philosophy and religion. I now offer a brief sketch of that history.

Philosophy and Religion: A Brief Historical Sketch

Ancient Philosophy

Ancient Philosophy arose as an attempt to say literally what Greek folk religion was saying in other ways. Against the background of poetic constructions (Hesiod's *Theogony*), the Ionian cosmologists attempted to give a more literal, proto-scientific account of the world. Later the focus shifts from cosmology to humanity, with Socrates insisting that "the proper study of mankind is man." As we learn in *The Apology,* Socrates alienated supporters of Greek folk religion in so doing. During this period, philosophy emerges as an attempt to break away from poetic and religious attempts to understand the world to develop a more literal, rational understanding. Plato's conception of The Good will have its measure of influence on the Augustinian and Platonists conception of God, and the Unmoved Mover that appears in Book 7 of Aristotle's *Physics* is thought to be the prototype for Aquinas's "proofs" for the existence of God.

Medieval Philosophy

In this period, philosophy is construed as the handmaiden of theology. The operant phrase might be: *Fides quarens intellectum* ('faith seeking understanding"). The great scholastic systems emerge from Albertus Magnus, Thomas Aquinas, Duns Scotus, William of Occam. In this period, philosophy plays a subservient role to religion; the task of philosophy is to provide a foundation for theological inquiry. Two notes bear on future developments. First, in this period, we have the development known as fideism, which springs from Tertullian's *"Credo quia absurdum"*—a statement that has been easily misunderstood and ridiculed. What Tertullian's statement means is that because it is paradoxical, a mystery, Christianity cannot be understood: one's relation to it is different; faith is not an intellectual relationship to a proposition, but rather a relation to the God-man (a paradox). Second, Anselm presents his ontological argument for the existence of God; Aquinas' so-called proofs for the existence of God occur in the *Summa Theologiae* in the context of his theological work, where they are called *"viae,"* not proofs.

Modern Philosophy

In modern philosophy, a distinct shift begins with Descartes who, while retaining a connection with religion and theology, nevertheless wants to abandon the scholastic infrastructure. Descartes wants to "start over," now using mathematics and the newly emergent sciences as models for inquiry, stressing the need for knowledge as incorrigible, certain and systematic. Proofs of the existence of God and immortality remain as important items on the agenda: the task of philosophy is to prove what otherwise is taken on faith. This same set of issues is taken up by Locke on the so-called empiricist side, and now we have the setting for the dialectic of modern philosophy--the debate between rationalism and empiricism about the origins, the nature and the extent of human knowledge. We cannot follow all the details but clearly philosophy stands related to religion. For example, all of the important philosophers of this period take up the God-question. For Descartes, God is infinite substance; for Spinoza, God is Nature (pantheism); with Leibniz we have the origins of theodicy—the attempt to justify the ways of God to man. Locke is concerned to demonstrate the reasonableness of Christianity; Berkeley wishes to eliminate matter because he sees belief in matter as an obstacle to faith; and with Hume's criticisms of the argument from design in *Dialogues concerning Natural Religion,* philosophy arrives at its skeptical moment.

The final two chapters in modern philosophy occur with Kant and Hegel. Kant (1965) says in *The Critique of Pure Reason,* that he found it necessary to set limits to reason in order to make room for faith. He argues there that reason winds up in contradictions when it attempts to demonstrate the existence of God; so the existence of God becomes a postulate of Pure Practical Reason. In Hegel, Christianity becomes one of many revealed religions whose presence Hegel seeks to explain as a manifestation of what he calls the Absolute. For Hegel, all reality is fully intelligible. Faith is a relative moment that must be transcended in the ascent of consciousness to Absolute Knowledge. Religion and philosophy have the same content but philosophy expresses it conceptually, whereas religion presents it symbolically, or in narratives. The Absolute can be seen as Hegel's philosophical surrogate for God.

In conclusion, we see that religion is absolutely central to the problematic of modern philosophy.

Postmodern Philosophy

The event that, more than any other, defines the postmodern period in European philosophy is Nietzsche's proclamation of the death of God. In this sketch, there is not time to rehearse the details of this proclamation. I confine myself to two points. First, Nietzsche's assassination does not exonerate atheism; the atheists are pictured as being just as clueless about this event as believers. Second, the thrust of Nietzsche's proclamation is to make philosophy autonomous, independent of God and religion, and to develop what might be called a *secular philosophy (The Gay Science, 1954).*

It is also important to take note of Kierkegaard's response to the Hegelian reinterpretation of God and religion. In *Philosophical Fragments*, (1941) he develops a view of faith and Christianity in which he aims to represent it in a way that is faithful to the experience of those who were contemporary (faith as contemporaneity with the Teacher) and which absolutely distinguishes Christianity from philosophy. Going against the trend in his times that sought to show the identity, or at least the continuity, of philosophy and religion, Climacus argues in "The Project of Thought" that philosophy (as represented by the Socratic moment) and Christianity are contradictory. To the question: How far does the Truth admit of being learned?" Philosophy says "all the way"; Christianity (the hypothesis in his Project of Thought) says "not at all."

20th Century Philosophy

It has become customary to divide philosophy in this period into Continental and Anglo-American philosophy. Let's look briefly at each in turn.

Continental Philosophy

Looking to the great philosophical systems that follow on Nietzsche, we look naturally to the work of Heidegger and Sartre. A secular philosophy emerges in *Being and Time* (1962) in which human reality (*Dasein*) is understood without any reference to God. In Sartre's *Being and Nothingness* (1958) likewise we encounter a philosophical system in which there is no God. There is only being-in-itself and being-for-itself, though the idea of God remains as an echo in the background when Sartre says that man is the being who desires to be god. Thus one might think that the God issue is not on the table. But that would be to overlook the work of those who constitute what has sometimes been referred to as the Christian wing of Existentialism: Unamuno, Marcel. In the latter half of the 20th century, one may cite Habermas as representative of the treatment of religion: there is none! (But see below, p. 126, for a refinement.) On the whole, then, we would have to say that the God issue is definitely in the background as far as the dominant developments in continental philosophy.

Anglo-American Analytic Philosophy

The central development in the first part of the 20th century is Pragmatism. Peirce is best known for his development of pragmatism and the pragmatic theory of truth. Less well known is the fact that Peirce was himself a believer and his faith plays a crucial–if unacknowledged role–in his philosophy.[1] James defended religion in various places, notably *The Will to Believe* (1896) and *The Varieties of Religious Experience* (1912), which Dennett cites widely. In addition we should take note of Process Philosophy and its interest in reconceptualizing God as process rather than substance. In American philosophy, as it develops after the war, Quine is, by almost all accounts, the most important philosopher, and his philosophy can well be described as secular: God and religion are non-issues on his philosophical agenda.

In England, the central development here is the issue of whether religious language is meaningful. In his *Language, Truth and Logic* (1936), Ayer presented his brand of empiricism—positivism—which sought to eliminate metaphysics and religion. The debate in the 20th century parallels that in the 19th except that the focus is not human mind and the extent of knowledge but rather (due to what has been called The Linguistic Turn in philosophy) the conditions of meaningful discourse. Ayer argues that religious propositions are nonsense: they are neither analytic nor empirical. This poses the problematic that follows: Can religious language be shown to be meaningful thereby meeting the challenge? In a famous symposium held in 1955, Antony Flew posed a crucial question: "What would have to occur or to have occurred to constitute for you a disproof of the love of, or the existence of, God"?[2] (1955,99). That debate about religious language comes to an end in the 60s; and the second half of the 20th century British philosophy develops without significant reference to religion.

To summarize, in the 20th century, philosophy achieved a kind of rough separation from religion of the sort anticipated by some 19th thinkers. There are hints of the emergence of secular philosophy, worked out very differently in Quine and Sartre. At the same time, religion continues to make its presence felt in the works of major philosophers, like Peirce, James, and Hartshorne. Still it seems clear that the philosophical agenda is differently ordered than in the postmodern era, in that the issues posed historically by God and religion are sidebars. They are not where the action is in either Continental or Anglo-American philosophy. But then comes 2001. Religion and the God issue once again become focal points, not because of any internal dynamic in philosophy, but rather because of events in the external world.

The New Atheism

An important cultural shift took place after 2001. Atheists came out of the closet, put on their gloves, and entered the arena. The "new atheism" emerged.[3] Some of the prominent documents mentioned above that illlustrate this shift are: Harris, *The End of Faith,* 2004; Dawkins, *The God Delusion,* 2006; Dennett, *Breaking the Spell,* 2006; Onfray, *In Defense of Atheism: The Case Against Christianity, Judaism, and Islam,* 2007; Stenger, *God: The Failed Hypothesis,* 2007; Hitchens, *god is not Great,* 2007.

What about this new atheism? In the past, atheists typically made their case by showing why the so-called proofs for the existence of God did not work. For example, in *Language, Truth and Logic* (1936), Ayer argued that the propositions that lie at the core of religion are (literally) nonsense. The proposition that God exists is not meaningful, being neither analytic nor synthetic. Ayer also made it plain that he himself was not an atheist nor an agnostic, because at the core of both of these positions lies the proposition that God exists. The theist, so says Ayer, affirms it; the atheist rejects it, while the agnostic says "I don't know." But, *eo ipso,* all agree that the proposition "God exists" is meaningful, which is precisely what Ayer denies. And if he is right, then the issue of God is a pseudo-issue. The old atheism (e.g., Ayer: *Language, Truth and Logic;* [1936]; Russell: *Why I am not a Christian* [1964]) revolved around a number of points:

- Critiques of proofs for the existence of God
- The argument against God from the existence of evil
- Critiques of belief and faith, especially as regards their meaningfulness

The New Atheism (Dennett, Dawkins et al.) works differently. It involves:

- Critiques of the proofs for the existence of God
- Proofs for the non-existence of God
- Critiques of faith and religion in terms of their perceived cultural effects

Most fundamentally, as Albert Mohler observes:

"It is not so much that Dawkins is attempting to convince believers that they should no longer believe in God. To the contrary, Dawkins is attempting a very different cultural and political move. He wants to make respect for belief in God socially unacceptable."[4]

This approach is combative and has proven to be as controversial among atheists and agnostics, as among theists.[5]

For perspective, it should be noted that there are scientists who defend Christianity: see Collins, *The Language of God: A Scientist Presents Evidence for Belief* (2006). And there are those inside the religious establishment who display a healthy critical sensibility about religion: see Kimball's, *When Religion Becomes Evil* (2004).

Responding to the New Atheism

Attacks on religion and Christianity are perfectly legitimate and have ample historical precedent. They are the current version of what Paul encountered when he preached a crucified Christ to the Greeks (an offense) and to the Jews (a stumbling block).[6] I side with Kierkegaard who holds that those who embrace Christianity must recognize that at its core lies a faith which, to the outsider, must appear foolish, scandalous, even irrational—and that the attempt to make it appear rational, reasonable, a good bet, the best hypothesis—all of these risk distorting its real meaning. There is then a *caveat* from Kierkegaard: He who defends Christianity betrays it.[7] Kierkegaard has in mind the earnest attempts on the part of philosophers—Locke's *On the Reasonableness of Christianity,* (1696) would be an example—to make Christianity reasonable, or the last phase in the development of Geist (Hegel). In the *Concluding Unscientific Postscript,* (1941) Kierkegaard's pseudonymous author, Johannes Climacus, satirizes such attempts: "...It is as if Christianity has been promulgated as a little system, if not quite so good as the Hegelian; it is as if Christ—aye, I speak without offense—it is as if Christ were a professor, and as if the Apostles had formed a little scientific society" (193).

I turn now to two samples from the literature of the new atheism. First, I review a line of argument that has had some play in many quarters. It takes the form of a recitation of the litany of horrors that can be attributed to religion. I will focus on the Dawkins version first. And then turn my attention to aspects of Dennett's indictment of religion in *Breaking the Spell*.

Problems with the Atrocity Calculus

Recall Dawkins version of the litany of horrors he ascribes to Christianity: "Imagine no suicide bombers, no 9/11, no 7/7, no Crusades, no witch hunts, no Gunpowder Plot, no Indian partition, no Israeli/Palestinian wars... no persecution of Jews as Christ killers..." The *implication* here is that, given all these evils/misdeeds committed in the name of religion, religion should be abandoned/banished. This is really not much more than the sketch of an argument which has not, by any means, been adequately developed, as those who invoke it must well know. But just in case someone might find this suggestion of an argument persuasive, I want to point to some potential problems with it. In any developed form of the argument, a number of considerations will have to have been addressed.

First, it will be necessary to ward off the challenges to the assumption that religion is the culprit behind these entries on the list of horrors, rather than its being one causal factor among others (politics, etc). Many have argued that the ongoing hostilities between Israel and the Palestinians are as much about land and politics as religion. Thus, in some cases, it may be problematic to attribute the atrocity primarily, or exclusively, to religion.

Second, Dawkins omits from his litany the "goods" that religion has been responsible for. One thinks, for example, of the prominent role in ending official discrimination played by the Rev. Dr. Martin Luther King Jr., Rev. Roy Wilkins and other ministers in the Southern Christian Leadership Conference. One thinks as well of the social gospel—the mandate to care for the poor, the oppressed, the downtrodden, and the many goods it has accomplished throughout the world. Think of Mother Teresa's work with the poor, but see Hitchens (2007) for another take on this. Think further of the role played by the Roman Catholic church and Pope John Paul II in breaking the hold of communism. If one is attempting to think critically about religion, then, *by all means, (pace* Hitchens) indict religion for the ills for which it has been responsible, but also, *by all means,* one must be prepared to praise it for the goods, *if the assessment is to be fair and rational.* [8]

Here we run into an important complication, for many of the goods that religion is associated with will not register on the world historical scale—in the same way that these alleged atrocities do. These are the "goods" referred to by William James in the famous passage from *Varieties of Religious Experience* quoted earlier: responses to prayers, conversations with the unseen, voices and visions, changes of the heart, deliverances from fear, infusions of help, as well as assurances of support.

These are often experienced without being voiced, or are voiced to only a few close friends and so do not come into view on the world historical radar scan. This is the point that Kierkegaard makes when he has Climacus argue in the *Postscript* that the world-historical is subject to a quantitative dialectic, but Christianity and the ethical are not; the dialectic there is qualitative. We are in the realm of inwardness and subjectivity. Yet if one is to engage in a calculus of the goods and evils associated with religion, this data would somehow have to be obtained. If Kierkegaard is right, then the sort of calculations Dawkins *et al.* have envisaged is vexed.

Third, Dawkins and others who have recited this litany fail to give serious consideration to the evils that have been perpetrated in the name of atheism: Marxism, Stalinism—both of which were to some degree "scientific" religions and which sought to extirpate religion—and religious believers:

> There is always the awkward reality that the 20th century regimes, officially and militantly atheist, committed atrocities on a scale never before conceived in history. On a slow day, the Stalin regime oversaw more executions than the Spanish inquisition carried out in four centuries. The same could be said of Lenin or Mao or Pol Pot. (Philip Marchand, *Toronto Star*, May 6 2007)

Finally, if by some "miracle" we could quantify the goods and the evils committed under the aegis of religion and those committed under atheism (or non-religion), we would still need a computational scheme, some way of integrating and computing all the data to determine which had achieved the better score. I know of no such scheme. Absent such a computational routine, an appeal to the atrocity calculus is a nonstarter.

Dennett's Critique

I turn now to Dennett's critique in *Breaking the Spell* partly because here we have the benefit of seeing how one of the best current philosophical minds comes to grips with religion and because Dennett is especially concerned with the future of religion (2006). Here I can focus on just two dimensions of this book: his rhetorical stance and his argumentation. Dennett presents himself as an open-minded philosopher concerned about the future of religion who wants to challenge believers to engage in a rational assessment. In the process he uses a number of rhetorical devices (tropes) that I want to call attention to.

The "Spell" Trope

The most obvious rhetorical device is the use of the word "spell" which appears in the title—*Breaking the Spell (2006)*—and again throughout Chapter 1. It would be easy to take immediate umbrage at his classifying religion as a spell, which connotes (black) magic and witchcraft, so it is important to understand that this is not the explanation that Dennett gives for his employment of the term, (though I think he trades on it). Dennett first invokes the term on page 12 where he is picturing someone at a concert when a cell phone rings and "breaks the spell." Here the word "spell' is being used broadly; it allows for both good spells and bad spells. Then Dennett recounts the Jonestown massacre and other examples of spells cast by religion. He adds that "religious cults and political fanatics are not the only casters of evil spells" (13)—implying thereby that they are among the casters of such spells. "The best way to break the evil spell is to introduce the spellbound to a good spell, a god spell, a gospel"(14). From these texts one can see that Dennett is getting a lot of mileage out of this trope. Dennett concedes that believers have a right to believe what they want, provided no harm is done, "[b]ut it is getting harder and harder to be sure about when this is the case… Eventually we must arrive at questions about ultimate values and no factual investigation could answer them"(14). In other words, questions about ultimate values are not scientific, and we need to have a clear account of the reasons that can be offered for and against the different visions [value schemes] of the participants. And those who refuse to take part in this process are part of the problem.

We come then to the sense in which the term "spell" is being invoked: "The spell that I say must be broken is the taboo against *a forthright scientific no holds barred investigation of religion as one natural phenomenon among many*" [emphasis added] (17). The term "spell" is not used to characterize religion itself but rather those religious persons who regard any criticism as sacrilegious. Religious believers are "under a spell" about their attachment to religion, and they systematically rebuff any criticism by attempting to cast a spell which renders it impervious. The spell trope is supported by another rhetorical device—the asymmetry thesis.

The Asymmetry Thesis

Dennett apparently believes that religious people generally resist criticism, whereas "atheists and scientists in general welcome the most intensive and objective examination of their views"(16).[9] Dennett believes that up to now there has been a largely unexamined mutual agreement that scientists and other researchers will leave religion alone (18). This is the asymmetry thesis: "The religious in contrast often bristle at the impertinence…the lack of respect, the sacrilege, implied by anybody who wants to investigate their views. I respectfully demur. This spell must be broken and broken now"(17).

There is certainly something to what Dennett is saying here: some religious people do react defensively to criticism. But many do not; many encourage and engage in such discussions. Certainly philosophers have not been cast under any such spell, for they have tackled religion forthrightly and regularly and mercilessly. Think of Voltaire, Marx, Nietzsche, Russell, and Sartre. But think also of the tradition of Christian apologetics: for example, C. S. Lewis's *Mere Christianity.* Think of the debates that took place on the BBC between Copleston and Russell (1945), and later Copleston and Ayer (1948).[10]

By the same token, one wants to ask: what is the evidence that atheists welcome such investigation? Is there any reason to believe that atheists are any more open-minded than theists? I know of no such evidence. In fact, consideration of the next rhetorical device will suggest the opposite. Some who are broadly sympathetic to Dennett's view have been put off by his attack: e.g., Michael Ruse.[11]

The "Bright's" Trope

In 2003, Dennett introduced the term "bright" to "draw attention to the efforts of some agnostics atheists and other adherents of naturalism to coin a new term for us non-believers." On page 21, he writes: "I am a *bright*" (21). What justifies the claim to being a bright is, apparently, not just that one is smart, but that that smartness has caused the individual to see through religion and reject it.

This *rhetorical* device caused a bit of a stir. Dennett was challenged about the implication of this choice of labels. Many objected to the apparent implication that those who choose religion are not bright, but dumb. In response, Dennett invoked the use of "gay" by homosexuals—a quite different situation—and denied that his intention was to imply that believers are stupid, suggesting that if they wanted to, those who believe could call themselves "supers." But why would someone who claims to be a follower of Christ want any other name? And did Dennett really think that the term "atheist" was on a par with "homosexual?"

Dennett says:

O religious folks who fear to break the taboo: Let go! Let go!... The sooner we set about studying religion scientifically, the sooner your deepest fears will be allayed. But that is just a plea, not an argument, so I must persist with my case. I ask just that you try to keep an open mind and refrain from prejudging what I say because I am a godless philosopher, while I similarly will do my best to understand you (20-21).

Here and throughout, Dennett presents himself as an open-minded inquirer from whom religious folks have nothing to fear. But the reader of *Breaking the Spell* will, at this point, have cause to wonder how open-minded Dennett really is, or whether he has not made up his mind just how the inquiry will turn out. I am reminded here of what James wrote in *The Will to Believe:*

The greatest empiricists among us are only empiricists on reflection: when left to their instincts, they dogmatize like infallible popes. When the Cliffords tell us how sinful it is to be Christians on such "insufficient evidence," insufficient is really the last thing they have in mind. For them the evidence is absolutely sufficient, only it points the other way (1896, 13-14).

On the whole, then, it seems to me that Dennett has made use of several questionable rhetorical devices to advance his position.

Problems with Dennett's Argumentation

Dennett calls for a scientific, rational examination of religion that will lead to an understanding of what purpose religion serves in our culture. He pleads for religions to engage in empirical self-examination to protect future generations from the ignorance so often fostered by religion hiding behind doctrinal smoke screens. But there are problems.

First, I have already commented on Dennett's definition of religion, cited earlier. Dennett appears to be going after theism—a philosophically worked-over version of Christianity. Belief is belief in God; there is no recognition of the difference between "believing that God exists" (as a kind of cosmological truth) and faith in Jesus Christ (as a personal decision). Dennett claims to have talked to many religious people but he does not appear to have read some of the most articulate proponents of the position he is criticizing. Kimball's *When Religion Becomes Evil* presents a much more sophisticated version of religion which would not be subject to Dennett's criticisms. I return to this point below.

Second, it is not clear what it means for religion to pass the science test. Most of the propositions of religion are propositions of value, or injunctions to behave in certain ways. Christians naturally orient themselves around such sayings as "Blessed are those who hunger and thirst for justice, for they shall be satisfied" (Matthew 5:6) and "I am the Way, the Truth, and the Life" (John 14:6). It is hard to see how these propositions, which are central to Christian faith, could be tested by science. To be sure, there are truths associated with religion but these are, I want to say following Kierkegaard, secondary.

Third, the principle of bilaterality would seem to suggest that if religion must pass the text of science, then science ought to pass the religion test. I take it that perhaps the principal task of religion is the setting forth of ultimate values by which people are expected to live their lives. Can science provide values by which a human can live a good life? The values promoted by science are chiefly epistemic; but any full human life is more than an epistemic undertaking. Where are love, charity, integrity? Interesting that Dennett himself at times proclaims sacred values. He writes that "life is sacred..." (22) But that is certainly not a view that emerges from a strictly scientific point of view, from the point of view of the evolutionary process, where, we are told time and again, the life of the individual means nothing. The species is what matters. Elsewhere Dennett (2006) writes:

> In spite of the religious connotation, even atheists and agnostics can have sacred values: values that are simply not up for reevaluation at all. I have sacred values in the sense that I feel vaguely guilty thinking about where they are defensible and would never consider abandoning them in the course of solving a moral dilemma (22).

He then presents his own list of sacred values: "democracy, justice, life, love, and truth" (23). But, pardon the expression, the devil is in the details. For these are nothing more than words until they are unpacked. Now what science are we to turn to that will provide an understanding of love or justice? Sociology? The value-free sciences? It seems clear that science cannot unpack these in any forceful way, so Dennett would have to rely on philosophy or literature. But we have already seen that traditional philosophy is heavily laced with religious content, and the question is whether a secular philosophy can provide the needed account. Nietzsche encountered a similar problem in *The Gay Science ("How Far We Too are Still Pious," #344)*

> But you will have gathered what I am driving at, namely, that it is still a *metaphysical faith* upon which our faith in science rests—that even we seekers after knowledge today, we godless ones and anti-metaphysicians still take *our* fire, too, from the flame lit by a faith that is thousands of

years old, that Christian faith which was also the faith of Plato, that God is the truth, that truth is divine.

The question is: What kind of account can be offered of these sacred values that does not itself depend heavily on these interdicted religious values?

Fourth, I want to press again the criticism that Dennett has not met his dialectical responsibilities. I refer now to his failure to address Kimball's views. In other places, I have argued that arguers have the responsibility to search out and deal with alternative positions (Johnson, 2000; 2006). In this regard, Dennett's argumentation is incomplete because he has not responded to the position taken by Kimball in which he addresses many of the issues and objections raised by Dennett. See, for example, his Chapter 1: Is Religion the Problem? One wants some sense of how Dennett would deal with a "more sophisticated" presentation of the religious perspective, as is required if one aims to undertake the kind of critical and open-minded examination Dennett claims to be engaged in.

These comments are meant to indicate some of the issues I found with Dennett's argumentation.

Conclusion

I have traced, in broad strokes, the relationship between philosophy and religion through its history. Philosophy is born out of religion; then in the medieval period becomes its handmaiden. In the modern period, philosophy may be described as striving for its independence, and in the last two centuries, to achieve autonomy. Only in the 20th century do we see the emergence of what might be called a truly secular philosophy (Sartre, Quine). This reading squares with the perception that results if we examine the major trends in philosophy in the 20th century:[12]

- the development of normative ethics in the wake of the withering away of positivism,
- the emergence of applied philosophy: applied ethics, bio-ethics, applied logic;
- the naturalizing tendency in philosophy and the decentering of epistemology;
- the emergence of neurophilosophy;
- the emergence of philosophy as critique of culture (Foucault and critical theory).

Now what is missing here? This agenda seems devoid of traditional philosophy's concerns with religion.

To be sure, there is still activity in that inquiry known as the philosophy of religion but the issues and debates here are not mainstream, as they were in the first half of the century. Then came 9/11; and mainstream philosophy, having all but discarded religion, finds that it must take religion seriously once again. And now it turns its venom on religion (Hitchens) (perhaps calling to mind Lear's lamentation: "How sharper than a serpent's tooth it is, to have a thankless child!") At the same time, it needs to be acknowledged that Christians have often been offensive in their promulgations, uncharitable in their actions and self-righteous, so when others criticize us, we need to listen carefully and learn what we need to learn, keeping in mind Matthew 5:38 ff.

What, in conclusion, can we say about the future of the relationship between philosophy and religion? In a way, the New Atheism can be seen as a reversion to an earlier view—a retro move, as it were. For it means that God and religion are back on the table for discussion: and had philosophy become truly secular, that would not have been the case. Religion is back on the agenda, not because the internal dialectic of philosophy has brought it back,[13] (as for example naturalized epistemology and neurophilosophy are clearly an outgrowth of the dialectic in philosophy in the first part of the 20th century) but rather because of philosophy's need to respond to developments in the world it seeks to render intelligible. There is nothing at all wrong with this development, since philosophy must respond to developments in the world and not just in philosophy. Indications are that religion will remain on the agenda for the 21st century, and that the relationship between philosophy and religion is likely to remain an uneasy one.

Notes

[1] Peirce himself had a mystical experience in 1892 and developed the first new proof for the existence of God: *'A Neglected Argument for the Reality of God'*, Collected Papers 6 456, 1908.

[2] Of course, the question needs also to be put to the nonbeliever: "What would have to occur or to have occurred to constitute for you a proof of the love of, or the existence of, God?"

[3] I thought I had invented that term as I puzzled over how to configure the views of Harris, Dennett et al. Dawkins et al. But it turns out to have been coined in 2006. http://www.damaris.org/content/content.php?type=5&id=508

[4] http://www.damaris.org/content/content.php?type=5&id=508

[5] See Ruse's response to Dennett, n.12 below.

[6] "But we preach Christ crucified, unto the Jews a stumbling block, and unto the Greeks foolishness." 1Corinthians 1:23.

[7] From *The Sickness Unto Death*: "One sees now how extraordinarily (that there might be something extraordinary left)—how extraordinarily stupid it is to defend Christianity, how little knowledge of men this betrays, and how truly, even though it be unconsciously, it is working in collusion with the enemy, by making of Christianity a miserable something or another which in the end has to be rescued by a defense. Therefore it is certain and true that he who first invented the notion of defending Christianity in Christendom is *de facto* Judas No. 2; he also betrays with a kiss, only his treachery is that of stupidity. To defend anything is always to discredit it. Let a man have a storehouse full of gold, let him be willing to dispense every ducat to the poor—but let him besides that be stupid enough to begin this benevolent undertaking with a defense in which he advances three reasons to prove that it is justifiable—and people will be almost inclined to doubt whether he is doing any good. But now for Christianity! Yea, he who defends it has never believed in it."

[8] Most of the critics can see only the harms, the evil, and none of the goods; and most of the defenders can see only the good, ignoring of the harms. But this is precisely the path taken by uncritical thinkers. To think critically about a phenomenon, one must be prepared to assess both strengths and weaknesses. See Johnson (1992).

[9] For a competing view by a respected philosopher of science, see Feyerabend (1975).

[10] Retrieved from http://evans-experientialism.freewebspace.com/copleston.htm

[11] Many otherwise sympathetic atheists and agnostics have critiqued the antagonistic rhetoric of the 'new atheists'. In February 2006, agnostic Darwinist Michael Ruse had an ill-tempered exchange of e-mails with Dennett in which Ruse complained that Dennett's book *Breaking the Spell* is 'really bad and not worthy of you." Michael Ruse, www.uncommondescent.com/archives/844.

[12] This list is going to be controversial. Others would index the developments differently.

[13] Just after I completed this paper for the conference, Dr. Carol Stanton was kind enough to give me her copy of The *Dialectics of Secularization* which records an exchange between Jürgen Habermas and Joseph Ratzinger, then-cardinal of the Roman Catholic Church and later to become Pope Benedict XVI. The editor of this volume says that in his Frankfurt acceptance speech in 2001, Habermas, who describes himself as a follower of Max Weber in the sense that he sees himself as 'tone deaf in the religious sphere,' "surprised many people by demanding that the secular society acquire a new understanding of religious convictions which are something more and other than a mere relic of a past with which we are finished" (Ratzinger & Habermas, 2006: 13).

References

Ayer. A.J. (1936). *Language, truth and logic.* New York: Dover.
Brent. J. (1993). *Charles Sanders Peirce: A life.* Bloomington, IN: Indiana University Press.
Carter, S. (1993). *The culture of disbelief: How American law and politics trivialize religious devotion.* New York: Basic Books.
Collins, F.S. (2006). *The language of God: A scientist presents evidence for belief.* New York: Free Press.
Dawkins, R. (2006). *The God delusion.* New York: Houghton Mifflin
Dennett, D. (2006). *Breaking the spell: Religion as a natural phenomenon.* New York: Viking.
Feyerabend, P. (1975). *Against method: Outline of an anarchistic theory of knowledge.* Atlantic Highlands, NJ: Humanities Press.
Flew. A, (1955). *Theology and falsification.* In: Antony Flew and Alistair MacIntrye (Eds.), *New essays in philosophical theology,* 96-98. London: SCM Press.
Habermas, J., and J. Ratzinger, (2006). *The dialectics of secularization: On reason and religion.* (W. Schuller, Ed.; Brian McNeil, Trans.) San Francisco: Ignatius Press.
Harris, S. (2004). *The end of faith.* New York: W.W. Norton.
Heidegger, M. (1962). *Being and time.* J. Macquarrie and E. Robinson (Trans.). London: SCM Press.
Hitchens, C. (2007). *god is not great.* Toronto: McClelland & Stewart.
James. W. (1896/1956). *The will to believe & other essays.* New York: Dover.
—. (1902). *The varieties of religious experience.* New York: The Modern Library.
Johnson, R. (1992). The problem of defining critical thinking. In: S. P. Norris (Ed.). *The generalizability of critical thinking*, 38-53. New York: Teachers College Press.
—. (2000). *Manifest rationality: A pragmatic theory of argument.* Mahwah, NJ: Lawrence Erlbaum.
Kant, I. (1965). *The critique of pure reason.* N. K. Smith (Trans.). New York: St. Martin's Press.
Kierkegaard, S. (1941). *Philosophical fragments.* W. Lowrie, (Trans). Princeton: Princeton University Press.
—. (1944). *Concluding unscientific postscript.* W. Lowrie, (Trans.). Princeton: Princeton University Press.

—. (1941). *Training in Christianity*. W. Lowrie, (Trans.). Princeton: Princeton University Press.
Kimball, C. (2004). *When religion becomes evil*. San Franscisco: Harper.
Locke, J. (1696). *The reasonableness of christianity*. London:Awnsham and John Churchill.
Nietzsche, F. (1954). *The gay science. In: The portable Nietzsche*, W. Kaufmann (Trans. and Ed.) New York: Viking Press.
Onfray, M. (2007). *In defense of atheism*: *The case against Christianity, Judaism, and Islam*. J. Leggatt, (Trans.) Toronto: Viking.
Otto, R. (1967). *The idea of the holy*. Oxford: Oxford University Press.
Russell, B. (1964). *Why I am not a Christian*. London: Allen & Unwin.
Sartre, J.P. (1958). *Being and nothingness*. Hazel Barnes, (Trans.). London: Routledge.
Stenger, W. (2007). *God: The failed hypothesis*. New York: Prometheus Books.
Taylor, C. (2002). *The varieties of religion today*. Harvard: Harvard University Press.
Williams, P. (2007). *The new atheism*. Retrieved March 2007 from Culture Watch
http://www.damaris.org/content/content.php?type=5&id=508
Wittgentsein, L. (1953). *Philosophical investigations*. G.E.M.Anscombe, (Trans.) Oxford : Basil Blackwell.
—. (1967). *Zettel*. G.E.M. Anscombe, (Trans.); G.E.M. Anscombe, and G.H. von Wright (Eds.). Oxford: Basil Blackwell.

CHAPTER EIGHT

ISLAM AND MODERNITY

MOHAMMAD SADEGH ZAHEDI

Introduction

Although the West is the cradle of modernity, the phenomenon of modernity has transcended geographical borders, and now its achievements can be seen all over the world. During recent centuries, modernity has reached far and wide. One of the major differences between the experience of the modern era by Westerners and non-Westerners is that modernity has its roots in the West, but its fruits have reached all parts of the globe. Industrialization, modern structures of government, a market economy, technology and so on are the achievements of modern science and philosophy which first emerged in Western societies. However, modernity has taken a different course in other parts of the world. In some of those parts, people have first come to know the superficial levels of modern achievements before penetrating to deeper levels. Muslims are no exception to that rule. This issue has given rise to questions about the relationship of modernity with non-Western cultures and societies.

Muslims have come to know modernity over the past two centuries. The Muslim world's knowledge about modernity has become more profound during those years, and the relationship between Islam and modernity has been one of the main concerns of Muslim thinkers. Many factors were influential in introducing Muslims to Western civilization, including colonialism by the West as well as the migration of Muslims to Western countries. Colonialism, which introduced modernity to Muslims, on the one hand, and deepening knowledge of Western countries about Islam, on the other hand, led to the emergence of new academic courses in Western universities on what came to be called "Orientalism." Although the Islamic and Western worlds had significant contact many years before the age of colonialism, (especially in the 7th and 8th centuries A.D. just after the advent of Islam) a new element that emerged in the early 19th century is what has been described by Edward Said (1994) as modern

Orientalism. Modern Orientalism is the result of efforts made by modern Westerners to know Islam and Muslims in modern times and on the basis of the paradigm of modernity. It has seen many ups and downs during the past centuries, and today, few researchers can call themselves true "Orientalists." Even such phrases as "specialist in Islam" or "specialist in Iran" are no longer academically valid terms due to the specialization of academic studies in our times. As Said has noted when describing modern Orientalism, Islam and Islamic culture have been considered by Orientalists as "the other." By presuming that modernity is superior, and influenced by the background of cultural and religious notions of classic Christianity, modern Orientalists have based their understanding of Islam and the Islamic civilization on a clear demarcation between "insider" and "outsider." Such a division applies to geographical, ideological and cultural features. Of course, Said's analysis of modern Orientalism has its own critics (Turner 1994), and Said himself has noted that all Orientalists are not similar and offer a wide spectrum of ideas.

Since the second half of the 20th century, and since the acceleration of globalization which has almost erased geographical and cultural borders, and especially after the emergence of postmodernist viewpoints which challenge the superiority of modernism, new hopes were raised that the analysis of Islam on the basis of "insider" and "outsider" categories would change. Other elements that many hoped would contribute to a new perspective include: the increasing number of Muslim citizens in Western societies; and the notion of a "global" perspective that would facilitate cooperation and mutual understanding among religions and cultures.

However, analyses that use categories such as "clash of civilizations," and events like the terrorist attacks of September 11, 2001, have reinforced the old cliché of "insider" and "outsider." Today, Western societies, especially their universities are eagerly seeking more information about Islam, but this trend is threatened by pessimistic interpretations and misunderstandings of Islam. In addition, the determinative role of the media in promoting anti-Islam viewpoints should not be overlooked. However, young students of Islam in the West still have the opportunity to avail themselves of the results of two centuries of intellectual endeavours by Western researchers.

What I seek to analyze here is not related to attitudes of Western researchers to Islam, but pertains to different approaches taken by Muslim scholars when confronting modern civilization. Apart from what Said says about the issue of "the other" in Orientalism, this issue is also faced by Muslims, though in a slightly different manner. As indicated above, the relationship between Islam and modern civilization has been one of the main concerns of Muslim thinkers during the past two centuries. The beginning of postmodernism has prompted some Muslim thinkers to talk about the situation of Islam in postmodern times and the relationship between Islam and postmodernism (Ahmad 2002). Understanding the relationship between Islam and postmodernism undoubtedly hinges upon understanding its relationship with modernity. At the same time, criticism of modernity does not necessarily mean that such criticism would benefit understanding Islam. If we consider one of the main claims of postmodernism to be a negation of the superiority of any meta-narrative, then it does not seem that there is any significant difference between the meta-narrative of Islam and that of modernity from a postmodern viewpoint. For now, let us set aside the controversial debate about the relationship between modernism and postmodernism and also between Islam and postmodernism, and focus on the main issue with which the Islamic world is currently faced; that is, the relationship between Islam and modernity.

Islam and Modernity: A Historical Review

As said above, the Islamic world first experienced the fruits of modernity through colonialism. On the one hand, the entry of Westerners into Islamic lands was heralded by their military power and modern arms which established their military superiority. This was the first time that Muslims were faced with weapons which looked new to them. Apart from establishing the superiority and power of Western armaments, the new weapons amazed non-Westerners More importantly, Westerners who had ventured into the Islamic lands with slogans about developing those lands and improving living standards of Muslims, brought new technologies with them. On the other hand, the industrial revolution had led to social welfare developments in the West. Muslims who had traveled to Western countries noticed improved sanitation, education and living standards of people in Western countries, and so they started to compare these developments to that of Muslim societies.

At first, Muslim societies admired the achievements of Western civilization and did not see religious implications in accepting them. However, discussions about the reasons for the "backwardness" of Muslims were raised, and the analysis of those reasons led to further discussions about the relationship between Islam and modernity and also drew attention to the roots of Western civilization and the theoretical bases of modernity. During this same period, cultural and economic elements in Islamic societies, attracted to modernity, were rapidly moving toward modernization. Efforts made at modernizing Islamic societies overlooked the cultural and ideological roots of these societies which then resulted in the emergence of conflict between the traditional and the modern. Thus, critical and even negative approaches emerged in tandem with the early sympathetic approach to modernity and Western civilization. Factors which should not be ignored here are the interaction between Western societies and Muslim nations as well as the effect of critical viewpoints which appeared in the West, especially the impact of Marxist thought on some Muslim thinkers. In this way, the "other" with which Muslims had sympathized at first, was later criticized and even negated (Enayat 2005).

The different approaches to the relationship between Islam and modernity in the Islamic world, can be divided into two broad categories: 1) thinkers who totally supported modernity, negated Islam and maintained that discarding Islamic ideas and adopting the values of modernity was the main way for Muslims to end their misery; 2) thinkers who were sympathetic to Islam and who tried to develop an Islamic approach for addressing the problems faced by Muslim societies (after confronting the modern world). The first group can be subdivided into rightist and leftist trends, with tendencies either toward liberalism and capitalism, or toward Marxism and socialism. The second group can also be subdivided into three smaller groups which include Muslim modernists, Muslim traditionalists, and Muslim fundamentalists. This chapter aims to analyze theoretical currents which tried to face modernity through an Islamic approach, and to enumerate their strengths and weaknesses. Such trends are also known as movements which aim to revive Islam.

Islamic Modernism

It seems that thinkers are unanimous about the fact that the modern era brought with it certain values which differentiate it from other eras of human history. If we accept that the pre-modern world based its values and legitimacies on religion, (which has given way to autonomous human reason in the modern world) we could then conclude that those earlier religious values raise the most important challenge between religious thought and modernity. The encounter between Christian thinkers and modern thought, and the efforts made to determine the relationship between Christianity and modernity has a long history. Those efforts were most obvious when they applied to public life. The difference between religious and secular ethics, as well as, between secular laws and religious teachings, are among the most prominent examples of such challenges.

Democracy is the most important political concept emerging in modern times. When it comes to the cultural and human aspects of modernism, natural laws and freedom are important concepts brought about by modern times. In addition, the new sciences which gave rise to modern technologies also brought with them a special worldview, which was different from what religion held about the world. Discussions in modern times led to debates on the relationship between science and religion or modernity and religion. The above developments show that modernity and its scientific and philosophical achievements have preoccupied religious thinkers as a theoretical issue. As modernity was introduced into the Islamic world, this issue also preoccupied Muslim thinkers.

Efforts made by Muslim thinkers to reread and reinterpret the Islamic texts were aimed at reconciling modern and Islamic concepts. One of the main components of Islamic modernism has been the recognition of new sciences. The first generation of Muslim thinkers endeavoured to show to Muslims that the new sciences and Islam were compatible. However, more philosophical and theoretical topics eventually came into sharper focus. For this reason, later works of such thinkers are attentive to such issues as Islam and democracy, Islam and human rights, as well as Islam and personal freedom. Seyed Jamaleddin Asadabadi (1839-1897), Seyed Ahmad Khan Hindi (1817-1898), Eqbal Lahori (1877-1938), and Mohammad Abdoh (1849-1905) are among the pioneers of this modernistic approach in the Islamic world.

Islamic modernism is an elitist movement, which sympathizes with modern values. While recognizing modernity, it tries to find an answer to the questions of how one can be a modern Muslim and how there can be a modern Islamic society. The Islamic modernist movement has progressed in parallel with a *secular* modernist movement in the Islamic world over the last century and a half. While secular intellectuals are unanimous in their belief that Islam and Islamic law are obstacles on the way to modernism in Islamic societies, modernist Muslims have taken a different approach in projects that simply aim at modernizing Islam. Correcting the belief system of Muslims, understanding Islam on the basis of new scientific and philosophical findings, and emphasizing "ijtihad" (extracting answers to new questions from Islamic sources)—all these efforts, have aimed to address the above issues.[1] Muslim modernists are fortunate to be able to draw upon the insights gained from the corresponding confrontation between Christianity and modernity. However, it should be noted that Islam's confrontation with modernity would not necessarily be the same as the Christian experience. Suffice it to say that the modernist movement is indeed raging in the Islamic world, and today a great number of researchers are studying the relationship between Islam and modernity.

Islamic Traditionalism

To the extent that Islamic modernists are sympathetic to modernity and modern ideas, Islamic traditionalists are critical of them. Since these modernists take a pluralistic approach to the truth of other religions and consider one single core for all of them, it has caused Islamic traditionalism to look upon Islam not simply as a source of identity for Muslims, but as a tradition which can save Muslims. For this reason, most attention has been paid by traditionalists to the spiritual aspects of human life, which, they believe, have been willingly or unwillingly marginalized as a result of modernization. Traditionalists maintain that due to an ontological reduction of human life to its physical aspect, modernity has caused humans to be distanced from truth, and thus they do not achieve their true status. Moreover, they believe that technology has greatly damaged nature, and the modern belief of ownership of the world among modern human beings has dealt irreparable blows to human nature as well as to nature in general. Traditionalists believe that modernity has destroyed the natural world and undermined human values by taking a mechanical approach to the world, which it sees only in quantitative terms, with no respect for spirituality (Nasr 2000). Major Muslim traditionalists include Frithjof Schuon (1907-1998), René Guénon (1886-1951), Martin Lings (1909-2005), and Seyed Hossein Nasr (1933-).

Although the traditionalists' perspectives draw attention to the damages inflicted by modernity, traditionalism is faced with the difficulty that it basically has no clear definition of tradition. Tradition is such a broad concept that it contains both the negative and positive values of the past, while lacking a selective and critical approach to those values. Furthermore, traditionalists reject modern reason, and talk about another form of intellect which is more inclined to understand than to criticize. Yet, they have never presented a clear definition of that intellect. At the same time, traditionalism lacks a consolidated and concrete plan to delineate future outlooks for Muslim countries. Just saying that we must find another definition for experimental science which would be based on a spiritual picture of the world, or just claiming awareness of the *Philosophia Perennis* which is transmitted by all traditions based on divine revelations would lead to salvation, may constitute moral advice but cannot be taken as a sufficient basis for the movement of Muslim societies into the rapidly progressing world of today. How can one avail oneself of modernity's human achievements while claiming that modernity itself is basically illegitimate? The existing shortcomings of the modern world have been noticed by modernists too, but this has not culminated in rejecting the positive achievements of modernity (Legenhausen 2005).

It should be noted that although Islamic traditionalism shares its critical viewpoint of modernism with Islamic fundamentalism, it does not go beyond Islamic ideology, and thus it should be differentiated from Islamic fundamentalism. Traditionalism takes a radically critical approach to modernity; however it cannot be considered a *radical* social movement. Rather, this radical approach to the modern world is primarily a feature of the Islamic fundamentalist movement.

Islamic Fundamentalism

Arguments about the necessity of going back to basic principles of religion have a long record among Muslims. Many Muslim thinkers and scholars have paid attention to these issues faced by Muslims since the early centuries after the demise of the Prophet Mohammad and have offered a way out. Perhaps the most famous of these is Abu Hamid Imam Muhammad Ghazali (1058-1111). He maintained that after the demise of the Prophet, Muslims had distanced themselves from his teachings. It was for that reason that he wrote his famous book, *The Revival of the Religious Sciences* (Al-Gazali 1986). The idea of a revival of religious sciences, in turn, inspired later Muslim scholars. Their presumption was that the Islamic society had distanced itself from the spirit of Islam and the teachings of the Prophet, and that a solution needed to be found to save Muslims. The common feature of all those currents was an internal criticism of the Islamic society based on Islamic principles. Islamic fundamentalism shares common ground with reformist currents in the history of Islam in that it believes that Islamic societies are constantly declining, and that this decline stems from Muslims ignoring Islamic teachings. However, there are basic differences between the two movements.

Fundamentalism in the world of Islam is considered a modern phenomenon rather than a traditional one, and it derives from a critical and negative approach taken to modernity in the Islamic world. Islamic fundamentalism places more emphasis on the need to protect Muslims' identity in the modern world and, thus, assumes an ideological aspect. Since the issue of identity is closely related to the appearances of religion, Muslim fundamentalists place special emphasis on the need to observe religious law. They claim that the main reason for the backwardness of

Muslim societies is inattention to the implementation of Islamic law in Islamic society, and that all efforts made by Muslims should be centered on that point. Muslim fundamentalists consider the implementation of Islamic law to be the most basic task of governments. However, it should not be assumed that other aforesaid movements do not stress religious law; both modernists and traditionalists regard Islamic law as part of valid religious teachings. The difference is that fundamentalism reduces religion to Islamic law. Perhaps it would not be erroneous to claim that fundamentalism pursues religious formalism. The appearance and lifestyle of Muslims, on the one hand, and presenting an interpretation of Islam according to which Muslims should under no conditions, be dominated by non-Muslims, on the other hand, has highlighted the xenophobic aspects of fundamentalism. Major fundamentalist figures in the Islamic world include Seyed Qutb (1906-1966), Rashid Reza (1865-1935), Abul Ala Maududi (1903-1979) and Abdul Salam Faraj (1952-1982).

Fundamentalism in Islamic countries, then, is a movement which is more of a social reaction than one rooted in powerful, theoretical premises. This movement places excessive emphasis on the appearance of religion, and other aspects of religion are treated with the same tunnel vision. However, this movement seems to appeal to Muslims who seek a haven, in the face of the onslaught of modern values, to protect their identity and to relieve themselves from the burden of thinking.

Due to the existence of various approaches in the Islamic world to modernity, when talking about the relationship between Islam and modernity, we must carefully explain the approach to which we refer because Islam can be interpreted in different ways. When discussing the relationship between Islam and modernity, reducing Islam to any one of those currents and overlooking the existence of different viewpoints in the Islamic world, leads to a misunderstanding of what is currently happening in Muslim countries. In addition, our analysis of the relationship between Islam and modernity must pay attention to different concepts of modernity. Modernity can be defined in political, cultural, economic, legal and cognitive terms. Since its inception, modernity has been a carrier for varied and even conflicting ideas, concepts and schools of thought. Therefore, care should also be exercised when discussing modernity. Just as liberalism is a modern idea, Fascism, too, is a spinoff of the modern world. The same is true about such wide-angled concepts as Socialism, Marxism, and Capitalism, all of which are products of the modern era. Even after this short description of existing trends in the Islamic world, which seeks to address the current situation for Muslims in their encounter with modernity, it seems that greater caution should be

exercised when talking about the relationship between Islam and modernity.
Muslim countries will need to tackle several problems before adapting to the modern world. The history of development in human societies clearly shows that theoretical and cultural changes are not brought about overnight; they need time. The experience of modernity in the Islamic world confirms that point. Social developments in Islamic societies have shown that overlooking religion or trying to phase it out of the social arena would not be helpful, and would only fan the flames of more radical tendencies. Islamic modernism has come about through the efforts of intellectuals who, on the one hand, maintain that the realities of the modern world are undeniable and, on the other hand, firmly believe that Islamic faith can survive in the modern world. However, such ideas have been limited to academic circles and have not penetrated the various levels of Muslim societies. Balanced growth and development of Muslim societies hinges upon the success of Muslim modernists to instil their ideas throughout the main body of Muslim culture. This is a general movement across the Islamic world, one which needs to be appreciated. Today, young Muslim researchers are offered various theoretical grounds that require serious discussion and deliberation. At present, vital topics do indeed enter into the discussion of the relationship between Islam and modernity in legal, economic, political, cultural, theological, and philosophical areas. Meanwhile, a critical approach to modernity taken by advocates of tradition as well as a sympathetic review of the experience of modernity in Western countries can also help solve many problems which Islamic countries are currently facing.

Notes

[1] There are famous contemporary modernist thinkers among them: Hassan Hanfi, Abdolkarim Soroush, Muhammad Arkon, and Nasr Hamid Abuzeyd who belong to the modernist current in the Islamic world.

References

Ahmad, A. (2002). *Islam and postmodernism*, London: Routledge.
Al-Gazali, M. Imam (1986). *Ihya ulum al-Din (Revival of religious sciences)*. Beirut: Dar al-Kotob al Elmiyah.
Enayat, H. (2005). *Modern Islamic political thought*. London: I.B.Tauris & Co., Ltd.

Legenhausen, M. (2005). *Siyahate andishe dar sepehre din (Voyage of reason in the sky of religion)*. Qom: Imam Khomeini Research Institute.
Nasr, S. (2000). *Islam and the plight of modern man*. ABC International Group Inc.
Said, E. (1994). *Orientalism*. New York: Random House.
Turner, B. (1994). *Orientalism, postmodernism and globalism*. London: Routledge.

AFTERWORD

RECENT DEVELOPMENTS IN PERSPECTIVES ON RELIGION

GREGORY BAUM

Introduction

In this chapter, I first discuss the religious events that have persuaded sociologists to abandon the theory of secularization which had predicted the end of religion under the conditions of modernity. Sociologists now recognize the important role played by religion, for better or for worse, in the contemporary world. Next I discuss the recent flourishing of religion, following that with some thoughts about the place of religion in Canada, arguing that there is currently no return to religion in the secular societies of Canada and Western Europe. Then I direct my attention to the impact of modernity on the Catholic Church.

The Theory of Secularization

The important sociologists of the 19th century argued that modernity was at odds with the inherited religion and would make it gradually disappear.[1] By modernity they meant democracy, industrialization and the predominance of scientific reason. Auguste Comte (1798-1857) proposed a theory of history in three phases. In the first phase, people explained the riddle of the universe in religious terms; in the second phase they turned to metaphysical explanations and abandoned religion; and in the third and final phase, people dropped metaphysics and relied exclusively on the empirical sciences to understand their place in the universe. Comte called his philosophy "Positivism." Two generations later, Émile Durkheim (1858-1917), one of the founders of scientific sociology, argued that the irrational beliefs of Judaism and Christianity would not survive in modern society. He made use of empirical research to demonstrate that people involved in industrialization and technology were gradually becoming indifferent to their faith: he showed that in the France of his day, men were less religious than women, people in cities less religious than people in the country, and working adults less religious than children and old people. In Germany, Max Weber (1864-1920) argued that the domination of techno-scientific reason produced by modernity would inevitably lead to the decline of culture and the waning of religion. While Comte gloried in the secularization of society, Weber lamented it, despite his personal indifference to religion: he spoke nostalgically of "the disenchantment of the world" (Weber 1958, 129-156). The American sociologist Peter Berger (1929-), himself a believer, still defended the theory of secularization in the 1960s. He changed his mind thirty years later.

The theory of secularization seemed to explain the growing indifference to religion in the industrialized countries of Europe. The wave of indifference became even stronger after World War II, possibly as a reaction to the Catholic Church's problematic relationship to European fascism: the concordat with Mussolini in 1929, the concordat with Hitler in 1933, the alliance with Franco in Spain and Salazar in Portugal, and during the war the support of Pétain by the majority of the French bishops. Even in Quebec, the hierarchy was largely suspicious of General de Gaulle's movement of resistance and favoured the Vichy regime in occupied France (Adams 2006, 54,120). Even though the Church changed its political sympathy after the war and favoured Christian Democracy, people tended to remain suspicious of the hierarchy. The Catholic Church paid a high price for its previous support of dictatorships.

What the theory of secularization was unable to explain was the thriving of religion in the United States of America. Alexis de Tocqueville marvelled at the vitality of religion on his visit to the United States in 1831; so did Max Weber on his visit in 1903. What has been the reason for this success?

It has been argued that the organization of religion in denominations was an original American creation that offered religious freedom to the entire population. On the European continent, the Peace of Westphalia of 1648 had decided that every society had its established Church, Catholic or Protestant, to which the population had to conform. Non-conformist Christians survived in small sects, aloof from their respective society. Yet in the United States, Christians organized themselves in denominations, thus moving beyond the difference between church and sect. Denominations resemble churches inasmuch as they support their society and cooperate with government to promote the common good. Denominations also resemble sects in as much as they see themselves as minorities, unable to represent society as a whole and thus reconciled to religious pluralism. Eventually even the Catholic Church in the United

States became a denomination in organizational terms. In the United States, Jews, Muslims and the followers of other religions were able to integrate into society because they organized themselves denominationally (Greeley 1972).

Another reason for the flourishing of religion in the U.S. may be the fact that the entire society was sustained by a religious myth, seeing itself as the New Jerusalem, the City on the Hill set up by God as an example to the nations. Robert Bellah (1974), who documented this civil religion in the 1960s, detected traces of it in the civil rights movement and in the student protest against the war in Viet Nam. Since the end of the 1970s, this civil religion finds expression in the right-wing Evangelicalism associated with the Republican Party.

We notice how different Canada is from the United States. While Canada never had an established Church, it did not produce the denominational system characteristic of the United States. In Canada, the majority of Christians belong to the three major Churches: Catholic, Anglican and United Church. In the United States, religion follows the pattern of free competition; in Canada, it is managed by three monopolies. Nor does Canada have a national myth to protect and promote its identity. I shall discuss the place of religion in Canada further on.

Recent Flourishing of Religion

I now turn to the historical developments that have persuaded sociologists to abandon the theory of secularization.

The East Asian Tigers

The successful industrialization in Japan has been imitated in a series of East Asian countries, South Korea, Taiwan, Hong Kong and Singapore. Because of their astounding economic achievement, they have been referred to as the East Asian Tigers. Today similar developments are taking place in China, India, Malaysia and Thailand. In all these cases, the industrial expansion is supported by a spirituality derived from the traditional religions. Since these religions promote what has been called a culture of harmony, the leaders in the East Asian countries have been able to interpret them as spiritual resources supporting "industrial harmony," the willing cooperation of workers with the demands made by management. Religion here plays a significant role in the industrialization of society.

Some sociologists regard this use of religion as a form of manipulation (Kinzley 1991). Yet there are other explanations. When Max Weber studied the East Asian religions, he concluded that they produced little energy for innovative social and economic developments. At the same time, Weber also demonstrated the creativity of religious traditions, the ability of religion to reread its sacred tradition and to promote a new kind of spirituality. It may well be, therefore, that the culture of harmony which currently supports the new economic development is sustained by an original development of the East Asian religions. What has been empirically demonstrated is that religious beliefs and practises have not declined in the East Asian Tigers.

This phenomenon has persuaded sociologists to explore the idea of "multiple modernities." While in the West the industrialization of society and the increasing reliance on techno-science have led to the secularization of society, there seem to be parts of the world where the process of modernization is sustained by the inherited religion. A turn to the Internet reveals a new literature on "multiple modernities" with reference not only to the East Asian Tigers but also to developments in Muslim countries and Latin America (Kamali 2000; Riedel et al, 2002).

The Pentecostal Movement in Latin America

Pentecostalism in Latin America is the fastest growing religion in today's world. At the beginning, the spread of Protestant populism in Latin America was supported by American funds intended to strengthen America's political influence on that continent. Yet since then, Pentecostalism has become a fully indigenous religious movement that responds to the needs of the poor people of Latin America. According to David Martin's *Tongues of Fire* (Martin 1990), Pentecostalism is successful because it combines two apparently irreconcilable tasks: on the one hand, it offers a modernizing spirituality fostering self-discipline, regular work habits and respect for women, the so-called Protestant ethic; and on the other hand, it provides an atavistic form of worship that allows the people to remember their indigenous past, speak in their half-forgotten languages and move in the rhythm of their ancient dances. More than that, Pentecostal congregations are self-help organizations that offer services to members and their families and help them to improve their standard of living.

There are structural reasons why the Catholic Church cannot compete with the Pentecostal movement. Pentecostal congregations are autonomous: The minister devises pastoral policies according to the needs and aspirations of his people. In the Catholic Church, by contrast, innovative pastoral approaches have to be approved by the bishop and in some cases even by Rome. When a Pentecostal minister meets an enthusiastic young man in his congregation, he gives him some training and sends him to another village to start his own congregation. A young man called to the priesthood in the Catholic Church will spend six years in the seminary, adopt the language of the educated and lose contact with the milieu from which he comes.

The Pentecostal movement among the poor of Latin America is not ecumenical; it defines itself in opposition to the Catholic Church and the traditional Protestant Churches. Because Pentecostal Christians tend to be upwardly mobile, many of them eventually move into the middle class, acquire advanced education, become entrepreneurs and aspire to political power that aims at transforming the culture of Latin America. There is no sign that this movement is abating.

The Awakening of Islam

To understand the new self-affirmation of Muslims, we must be conscious of the history of their colonization. In the 19th century European empires colonized Algeria, Morocco, Tunisia, Libya, Egypt and far away India; and after World War I, British and French mandates were established in Palestine, Iraq, Lebanon and Syria. It is not surprising that the Arabs looked upon the foundation of Israel as part of this colonising wave, while we, in the West, saw Israel as a house against annihilation, a refuge for a persecuted people. The Arabs struggling for political self-determination first adopted secular ideologies such as nationalism or socialism, yet when these failed to overcome their plight, they turned to their own cultural resources and declared that Islam was the solution. They passionately affirmed their Muslim identity. Over the last decades a religious awakening has spread across the Muslim world, moving beyond the Arab countries.

I use the word "awakening" to recall the Great Awakening in the British North American colonies of the early 18th century, a revival movement that embraced Christians from the various colonies and, as an unintended consequence, produced an awareness among Christians that they shared the same culture and in fact constituted a people. The Great Awakening was a prelude to the American Revolution (Cowing 1971).

The recent awakening of Muslims has produced diverse effects. It has persuaded ordinary Muslims to embrace their faith with joy, practise it more faithfully, become more visibly committed to their tradition and strongly affirm their religious identity. They do this even while living under conditions of modernity in cities all over the world. Yet there is also a conservative Muslim movement that is hostile to Western culture: This movement includes people we call fundamentalists, technically known as W*ahhabi*, who follow a rigid interpretation of Islam, refuse to dialogue with Muslims of the mainstream and uncritically reject all Western ideas. It is ironic that Wahhabism is promoted all over the world by Saudi Arabia with the oil money they receive from the West. Wahhabi Muslims long for an Islamic State. A small minority among them justifies the use of violence to achieve their political aim; they constitute a danger to the world.

The awakening of Muslims also includes reform movements that offer a humanistic reading of Islam. These movements have been a special interest of mine over the last two years. An important renewal movement began already at the end of the 19th century (Ramadan 1998). Jamal Al Afghani was a passionate critic of the conformism of Muslim societies, their neglect of public education, their refusal to foster the natural sciences and their passive submission to Western colonialism. Al Afghani denounced the folklorization of Islam: i.e., the integration into the faith of superstitions and cultural practices. He proposed instead a return to the Islam of the Prophet and his Companions that was capable of responding creatively to new historical challenges. Al Afghani's ideas were taken up by many Muslim thinkers and promoted by renewal movements in many parts of the world. Today there are Muslim theologians who offer an interpretation of the Qur'an and the Tradition that respects religious pluralism and encourages the co-responsibility of people for their collective well-being. (Roussillon 2005; Benzine 2004; Filali-Ansary 2003; Nader 2003; Ramadan 2004). Some of them regard themselves as strictly orthodox, while others—sometimes referred to as modernists—believe that the entry into modernity demands a break with the tradition. Reformist thinkers living in Muslim countries, including Iran, believe that the modernization of their society—pluralism and human rights—can be achieved on an Islamic basis.

Religious Identity Politics

The awakening of Islam has been the affirmation and defence of a collective religious identity. There are currently other religious movements that struggle to protect and enhance their identity.

The ancient Hindu tradition of tolerance is presently interrupted by a Hindu nationalist movement that protests against the secularism of the Indian State and is hostile to the religious minorities in India, especially Muslims and Christians. For students of Hinduism, such intolerance is an altogether puzzling development. One explanation is that the division of India in 1948 that produced massive violence between Hindus and Muslims has left unhealed wounds in Pakistan and the now-reduced India. More importantly, Hindus in India who constitute the great majority of the population are often critical of the secular constitution of their country. The Indian Constitution, based on Western models, defines the State as religiously neutral, forbids it to favour any particular religion, and yet demands that it defend people's religious liberty, especially the rights of minorities. Now, however, Hindus, the great majority, feel deserted by their government while Muslims, Christians and other minorities experience the government's protection. Hindu nationalists want a Hindu State, a government that promotes their religious culture and protects it from the influence of other religions and from the invasion of Western individualistic values. They are not against technology, science, industrialization and political parties, but they want an Indian form of modernity (Anderson 1998). While Hindu nationalism does not represent the majority of Hindus, it is a thriving political movement that is not likely to lose its political influence.

There are other religious movements that seek to protect a collective identity deemed endangered. More than that, religion is often instrumentalized by governments or political parties to legitimate policies of aggression and even to bless the use of violence. The civil war in Sri Lanka is a sad example of the manipulation of religion. A bloody conflict began in 1983 casting the government representing the Sinhalese community, 74% of the population, against the Tamil Tigers in the northeastern part of the island who were trying to set up an independent country. The Sinhalese people are Buddhists while the Tamils are Hindu. These two religions, famous for their spirituality of peace, are being used by political and religious leaders to justify the civil war, and to bless the use of violence.

A more peaceful contemporary example of identity politics closer to home deserves our attention. The Native Peoples of Canada continue to live in conditions defined by political colonialism. In recent decades, they have struggled to survive, to affirm their own culture and to obtain an appropriate form of self-government. To acquire a stronger sense of their own identity, the Native Peoples have turned to their own spiritual tradition, their beliefs and their rituals, which in the past had been denounced as pagan by the Christian Churches (Treat 1996). Today the major Churches have changed their mind: They regard Native spirituality as in harmony with the biblical doctrine of divine creation, and hence allow their Native members to integrate their rites and prayers into the official Christian liturgy. Yet there are groups of Native Peoples that are so angry with the culture and the religion imposed on them by the colonizing power that they prefer to opt out of Christianity and to define their identity in exclusive reliance on their traditional spirituality.

The place of religion in the industrializing nations of East Asia, the rapid spread of the Pentecostal movement in Latin America and other parts of the world, the awakening of Islam in its various forms and other religiously motivated identity struggles are major historical events that have convinced contemporary sociologists to drop the theory of secularization, recognise the ongoing vitality of religion, and to explore the emergence of multiple modernities.

Religion in Western Societies

In Canada and the countries of Western Europe, the secularization of society is continuing. Fewer people attend church services, fewer participate in the sacraments, and fewer make personal decisions for religious reasons. Religion appears less and less in public life; it is rarely invoked in political debates. Secularization is taking place in these countries at different speeds. The rate of secularization, as we shall see, is different in English Canada and Quebec.

Some sociologists attach great importance to the multiplication of new religious movements and centres of spirituality which cultivate inwardness drawing upon Eastern religions, Native spirituality, psychotherapeutic insights and ancient and new cultic practices (Clarke 2006). This development has convinced the British sociologist David Martin (2007) that spirituality or the quest for transcendence is a pursuit proper to all human beings, a pursuit that, in the past, had been channelled by the Churches and that, in the present, expresses itself in many different currents. Religion, Martin might say, has become deregulated. The absence of religion from people's lives, he thinks, is only apparent: In actual fact, religion is starting to thrive in alternative forms.

I am not persuaded by this argument. The new religious and spiritual movements involve a limited number of people. Statistically they constitute a marginal phenomenon in society. Moreover, according to Max Weber, religion is more than a current of spirituality: Religion is a powerful, culture-creating force that at one time moved through society and, in doing so, transformed it. For sociologists, religion is more than believing in God. Religion is both intimate and public: It warms the heart and incarnates a social vision. I am obliged to conclude that, despite the new religious movements, Western societies (apart from the United States) are experiencing a gradual secularization of their culture.

The ecological crisis and drastic economic decline may eventually change this! Since religion offers an ethos of self-limitation, people may turn to it as they are forced by the conditions of the environment to reduce their consumption and adjust to a simpler life style. Religion may also revive because in the misery and loneliness produced by chronic unemployment, parishes and congregations offer people solidarity and assistance in self-help undertakings. In my opinion, only dramatic occurrences of destruction will reveal to the West the folly of its cultural orientation toward "bigger and better" and persuade people to look for an alternative culture moderated by a transcendent element.

The Place of Religion in Canada

Quebec

Quebec is a special case of rapid secularization (Baum 1991, 15-47). Quebec was a province in which the Catholic Church had an extraordinary cultural power. In societies colonized by an empire of a different faith, the inherited religion becomes the symbol of resistance and survival. Ireland and Poland were such societies. Here religion thrives. In Quebec the Catholic Church also had an unusual institutional presence. Since there existed no ministries of education, public health and social work, the provincial government asked the Catholic Church to offer the services in these three areas to the Catholic population, the overwhelming majority. Especially during the regime of Maurice Duplessis (1936-1958), the premier used the bishops to reinforce conformity and obedience, and the bishops used the premier to promote their Catholic institutional preoccupations.

Starting in 1960, the political self-affirmation of the Francophone majority—the Quiet Revolution—challenged the power of the Anglophone economic elite, fostered the democratization of Quebec society and opposed the clericalization of public life. Since these were the years of Vatican Council II (which was redefining the Church's relationship to society), many Catholics, urged by their faith, participated in the cultural transformation and the declericalization of society. These Catholics did not foresee that the reaction against clerical power would rapidly lead to a drastic secularization of society. The Church lost its role in health care and social work, but retained a presence, although greatly reduced, in the school system. Within ten years, the Church was abandoned by two-thirds of its active members. Quebecers associated the Church with "*la grande noirceur*," an overblown reference to Duplessis' authoritarian regime and the priests' authoritarian control of their private lives.

While the Church that remains has many weary parishes, it is also a place of great vitality. In their pastoral statements the bishops of Quebec have been applying the teaching of Vatican II in a bold and imaginative way to the problems of society. They offer a progressive message on issues of social justice, religious pluralism, immigrants and refugees. A progressive Catholicism is being fostered in Quebec by movements, centres and reviews, supported by religious congregations and laymen and women.

The unexamined resentment against religion that still pervades Quebec society is presently prompting many people to react impatiently to the religious signs and symbols in which recent immigrants, especially Muslims, express their faith in the public sphere. In the debates on this issue, many Quebecers loudly insist that religion is a purely private matter that should be kept out of the public space. To calm their spirits and protect the immigrants, premier Jean Charest appointed a small committee to study the issue and make recommendation for the interpretation of the law. The nervous response of many Quebecers to the habits of strangers is also an expression of anxiety in regard to their own survival and identity, challenged as they are by the constant pressure exerted by the language and culture of the rest of North America.

English Canada

The secularization of society moves more slowly in English Canada. In Canada, religion has not followed the American pattern, as I stated previously. Since Canada did not separate itself from the British Crown by a revolution, the Canadian Churches saw themselves as extensions of European Churches, not as newly constituted bodies. The research of Bibby (2002) has shown that the gradual secularization in Canada follows the European pattern. In Canada, as in Britain, the attitude toward the Churches is increasingly polite indifference, rather than the resentment and anti-clericalism found in Catholic countries. Because the very foundation of Canada in 1867 demanded negotiation, compromise and adjustment, Canadians have developed a culture of moderation that even affects their religion. The Canadian Protestant theologian Douglas Hall has described American culture as confident, enthusiastic, and sometimes even messianic, while he sees Canadians as cautious and sceptical, avoiding extremes and moving to the middle. This also applies to Canadian

Christians who regard themselves as Evangelical. While they have recently become more numerous and exercise a certain cultural influence, they differ strikingly—as shown in a recent study (Reimer 2003)—from Evangelicals in the United States. The Evangelical Fellowship of Canada upholds a conservative personal morality, especially regarding issues of family and sex, very similar to that of the Catholic Church, yet on issues of democracy, pluralism and social justice it supports the middle-of-the-road mainstream of Canadian society.

A certain religious discourse has recently returned to political life among some members of the Conservative Party. These voices remain subdued. In Canada it may be a handicap rather than an advantage for a political party to make use of arguments drawn from religion. It is interesting that during the national convention of the NDP held in Montreal in 2006, a small group of members of Parliament, remembering the origin of CCF (the ancestor of the NDP) in the Social Gospel, called a meeting of party members who were socialists for religious reasons. Over two hundred people showed up. In my opinion, these are marginal events, important for the participants, yet not social indicators of a return to religion.

Despite the slow drift toward the secularization of Canadian society and the growing number of Canadians who define themselves as religionless, the Churches remain thriving communities, even if the active membership of the Catholic Church, the Anglican Church and the United Church is declining. Great vitality is also manifest in the non-Christian religious communities: Jewish, Muslim, Hindu, Buddhist, Sikh and Bahai. The multicultural policy of the federal government has provided security for immigrant communities. They feel that, despite occasional experiences of prejudice, their culture, including their religion, is officially respected.

The Catholic Church

I now want to explore what impact modernity has had on the Catholic Church and what problems modernity has created for it. In the 19th century, and earlier, the papacy condemned the liberal society that was then in the making. In the brief *Quod aliquantum* of 1791, Pius VI condemned the Rights of Man and the principles of the French Revolution. In the encyclical *Mirari vos* of 1832, Gregory XVI defended the feudal-aristocratic order and condemned democracy. In the encyclical *Quanta cura* of 1864, Pius IX condemned the principles of liberalism. In the encyclical *Libertas praestantissimum* of 1888, Leo XIII condemned civil liberties, including the freedom of religion. In the apostolic letter, *Notre charge apostolique* of 1919, Pius X condemned the Christian-democratic movement, Le Sillon, in France. This movement deserves condemnation, Pius X wrote, because it fosters the democratic education of the people: raising to its maximum the conscience and civic responsibility of everyone, and producing economic and political democracy and the reign of justice, liberty and fraternity.

Catholics living as minorities in the Protestant world, embarrassed by the Church's official teaching, were encouraged to demand religious liberty in their country for, in their situation, religious liberty served the spread of the true faith.

The Catholic Church redefined its relationship to modernity during Vatican Council II. I have documented this remarkable doctrinal development in a recent book called *Amazing Church* (2005). In the encyclical *Pacem in terris* of 1963, published during the Council, John XXIII endorsed the human rights tradition, including religious liberty on theological and philosophical grounds. Paul VI and John Paul II engaged in an open dialogue with modernity, supporting its democratic and emancipatory aspirations and, at the same time, deploring its promotion of individualism, utilitarianism and secularism. According to the Council and the popes, at this time the proclamation of the Gospel must include the call for human rights and social justice, and summon Christians to assume their social responsibility. Catholic social teaching has become audacious, supporting democracy and criticising capitalism. In fact, the Church's teaching rejects what it calls "liberal capitalism"—i.e., the unregulated market system—and demands that it be transformed into a market economy guided by rules and a spirit of cooperation, assuring that it serve the common good of society. John Paul II (1999) was boldly critical of today's globalisation of the free market system. Most Catholics do not realise that through the development of its social teaching, the Catholic Church has defined itself as a progressive force in today's world, promoting greater social and economic equality, and opposing the powers that generate injustice, oppression and wars.

Still, the encounter with modernity has created a problem for the Catholic Church which has as yet not been overcome, and which accounts, in part at least, for the conflict among Catholics and the fact that so many of them, including priests and religious, are walking away from the Church. A startling difference exists between the ethos of governance generated by modernity and the corresponding ethos in the Catholic Church. Catholics recognise that the Church is a hierarchical society founded upon the apostolic succession, yet as participants in modern society they expect an ethos of governance that includes consultation, transparency, open financial statements and independent courts capable of judging whether decisions of the hierarchy are in conformity with justice and ecclesiastical law. The present style of ecclesiastical government, however, still belongs to the feudal-aristocratic order. Catholics recognize the authority of the hierarchy, yet formed as they are by modern values, they expect a dialogical exercise of this authority and consider unethical the present style of ecclesiastical governance. The American bishops have acknowledged this conflict on one particular occasion. In their pastoral letter on economic justice, the bishops recognise the clash between the two styles of governance. They write:

> As we propose a new [economic] experiment in collaboration and participation in decision making by all those affected at all levels of U.S. society, so we also commit the Church to become a model of collaboration and participation (O'Brian 1992, 662, n.358).

Yet this collaboration never happened.

Invoking the concepts of collegiality and subsidiarity, the Second Vatican Council favoured a certain decentralisation of the Catholic Church. The Council recognised the co-responsibility of bishops for the Church universal; it established a world synod of bishops that would meet at regular intervals; it granted authority to national episcopal conferences to devise pastoral policies appropriate for their regions; and it recommended the creation, within the dioceses and the national Churches, of synods and councils that were to include priests as well as lay men and women. Yet subsequent measures taken by Rome have gradually reduced the authority of these institutions, and taken the Church back to a more monarchical style of government. Bishops are presently even asked to take a special oath that they will obey Vatican teaching. At this time, the Church's ethos of governance differs strikingly from the ethical ideals of modernity. What worries the sociologist is that the Church, because of the shortage of priests and religious, is being forced to close many of its institutions and interrupt many of its services, a worry that is as yet not shared by the hierarchy. They do not seem to look for imaginative ways of overcoming this problem.

It is not my intention here to study the Church's pastoral problems and or to examine the various ways that have been tried to overcome them. I have limited my attention to the impact of modernity on the Church, alluding first to its new critical openness to the social project defined by *liberté, égalité et fraternité* (*solidarité*) and, second, to the Church's inability to introduce the modern notion of social justice in its own self-organization. What makes the Church modern is also its international character, its global structure, its system of communication and authority that reaches across the continents, capable, at least in principle, of steering believing communities in all parts to foster, in the name of Jesus, cooperation, universal respect and peaceful resolutions of conflicts. That this does not always happen is only too well-known. The greatest assets of the Catholic Church are its sacramental gifts, especially the Eucharist, to which believers are deeply attached and from which they do not easily separate themselves, even if they disagree with certain ecclesiastical rules.

The flourishing of religion in Asia, Africa and Latin America under conditions of modernization—we have looked at this above—is not accompanied by a similar movement in Western Europe and Canada, except possibly in the United States. In the small book *Without Roots*, (2006) written by Benedict XVI, the distinguished author admits that a tired Church, weakened by secular values, cannot be awakened to new life from the top down, by the voice of the Pope and the bishops. The hope for the Church is located in "creative minorities." He writes:

> It is important to have convinced minorities in the Church [that], for the sake of the Church and society as a whole,…human beings, who in their encounter with Christ have discovered the precious pearl that gives value to all of life, are assured that the Christian imperatives are not a heavy burden that immobilizes humanity, but rather wings that carry it upward. Such minorities are formed when a convincing model of life also becomes an opening toward a knowledge that cannot emerge amid the dreariness of everyday life. Such a life choice, over time, affirms its rationale to a growing extent, opening and healing a reason that has become lazy and tired (120-121).

Conclusion

The predictions, on the part of several social sciences, concerning the imminent demise of religion have proven premature. There is an unpredictable quality both to the future and to humanity's religious behaviour that should prevent us from an overly pessimistic view. While we may not be able to articulate the particular features of religion's role in the culture in the years ahead, it seems quite likely, given the developments of the first decade of the 21st century, that religion will be part of it. Indeed it is already.

Notes

[1] I have examined these authors and discussed theory of secularization in my book *Religion and Alienation: A Theological Reading of Sociology*, 2nd edition (Ottawa: Novalis, 2006)

References

Adams, G. (2006). *Political ecumenism: Catholics, Jews and Protestants in de Gaulle's free France 1940-1945*. Montreal: McGill-Queen's University Press.
Andersen. W. (1998). Bharatiya Janata party: Searching for the Hindu nationalist face. In: H-G– Betz and S. Immerfall, (Eds.), *The new politics of the right: Neo–populist parties and movements in established democracies*. New York: St. Martin's Press.
Baum, G. (1991). *The church in Quebec*. Ottawa: Novalis.
—. (2005) *Amazing church*. Ottawa: Novalis.
Bellah, R. (1974). Civil Religion in America, In: W.G. McLoughlin, (Ed.). *Religion in America*. Boston: Beacon Press.
Benedict XVI. (2006). *Without roots*. New York: Basic Books.
Benzine, R. (2004). *Les nouveaux penseurs de l'islam*. Paris: Albin Michel.
Bibby, R. (1993). *Unknown gods:The ongoing story of religion in Canada*. Toronto: Stoddart
—. (2002). *Restless gods: The renaissance of religion in Canada*. Toronto: Stoddart.
Clarke, P. (2006). *New religions in global perspective: A study of religious change in the modern world*. London: Routledge.
Cowing, C. (1971). *The great awakening and the American revolution*. Chicago: Rand McNally.
Filali-Ansary, A. (2003). *Réformer l'islam?* Paris: La Découverte.
Greeley A. (1972). *The denominational society*. Glenview, IL: Scott, Foresman & Co.
John Paul II. (1999). *Ecclesia in America*. Apostolic Exhortation.
Kamali, M. (2000). *Multiple modernities, civil society and Islam: The case of Iran and Turkey*. Liverpool: Liverpool University Press.
Kinzley,W. (1991). *Industrial harmony in modern Japan. The invention of a tradition*. London & New York: Routledge.
Martin, D. (2007). The European model of secularization and its significance for Africa and Latin America. In: H. Joas, (Ed.).

Säkularisierung und die weltreligionen. Frankfurt am Main: Fischer Verlag.
—. (1990). *Tongues of fire: The explosion of Protestantism in Latin America.* Oxford, UK/Cambridge, MA, Basil Blackwell.
Nader, A. (2003). *Courants d'idées en Islam.* Montréal: Médiapaul.
O'Brian, D., (Ed.). (1992). Economic justice for all. In: *Catholic social thought.* Maryknoll, NY: Orbis Books.
Ramadan, T. (1998). *Aux sources du renouveau musulman.* Paris:Bayard.
—. (2004). *Western Muslims and the future of Islam.* New York: Oxford University Press.
Riedel, J. et al, (Eds.). (2001). *Reflections on multiple modernities.* Leiden/Boston: Brill.
Reimer, S. (2003). *Evangelicals and the continental divide.* Montreal: McGill-Queen's University Press.
Roussillon, A. (2005). *La pensée islamique contemporaine.* Paris: Théaèdre.
Treat, J., (Ed.). (1996). *Native and Christian: Indigenous voices on religious identity in the United States and Canada.* New York: Routledge.
Weber, M. (1958). Science as a vocation. In: H.H. Gerth and C.W. Mills, (Eds.) *From Max Weber: Essays in sociology.* New York: Oxford University Press.

CONTRIBUTORS

Gregory Baum, Th.D., is emeritus professor of McGill University, Montreal. He is an internationally renowned lecturer and the author of numerous books, including most recently, *Amazing Church* (2005).

Renée Bondy, Ph.D., is an instructor in the Women's Studies Program at the University of Windsor.

Stanley B. Cunningham, Ph.D., is emeritus professor of the University of Windsor having taught in both the Philosophy and Communications Studies Departments. He is the author of *The Idea of Propaganda: A Reconstruction* (2002) and *Reclaiming Moral Agency: The Moral Philosophy of Albert the Great* (2008).

Dennis Hudecki, Ph.D., is professor of philosophy at Brescia College, at the University of Western Ontario.

Ralph H. Johnson, Ph.D., is emeritus professor of philosophy at the University of Windsor and a Fellow of the Royal Society of Canada. He is the co-founder (with J. Anthony Blair) of the Centre for Research in Reasoning, Argumentation and Rhetoric and has authored 3 books and over 30 articles.

Charles Kimball Th.D., is an expert on Islam, the Middle East and Jewish-Christian-Moslem relations. He is currently Presidential Professor of Religious Studies at the University of Oklahoma. His book *When Religion Becomes Evil* was named one of the top 15 books on religion for 2002.

Donald Lococo, C.S.B., Ph.D., is a priest of the Congregation of St. Basil (Basilian Fathers) and a cell biologist holding the position of adjunct professor of biology at St. John Fisher College, Rochester, N.Y.

Moira McQueen, LL.B., Ph.D., is the Executive Director of the Canadian Catholic Bioethics Institute, and a member of the St. Michael's College Faculty of Theology, University of Toronto. Her most recent publication is *Bioethics Matters* (2008).

Paul J. Rennick, C.S.B., Ph.D. (Editor) is a priest of the Congregation of St. Basil and holds graduate degrees in both theology and psychology. He is currently the President of Assumption University, the founding university of the University of Windsor with which it is federated.

Carol Stanton, Ph.D., is a graduate of Trinity College, Dublin, Ireland and is currently the Co-Director of the Lay Ecclesial Ministry Formation Program for the Catholic Diocese of Orlando, Florida and Director of New Program Development for the San Pedro Spiritual and Leadership Development Centre.

Mohammed Sadegh Zahedi, Ph.D., is assistant professor of philosophy and theology at Imam Khomeini International University in Iran. His interests include comparative philosophy and theology and Islamic mysticism and the relationship between Islam and modernity.